BETTER THAN EVER

BETTER THAN EVER

Get Your Happy Back, Stress Less, and Enjoy Every Day

APRIL OSTEEN SIMONS

A POST HILL PRESS BOOK

Better Than Ever:
Get Your Happy Back, Stress Less, and Enjoy Every Day

ISBN: 978-1-64293-994-1
ISBN (eBook): 978-1-64293-995-8

Cover photo by Meshali Mitchell
Interior design and composition by Greg Johnson, Textbook Perfect

Post Hill Press
New York • Nashville
posthillpress.com

Published in the United States of America
1 2 3 4 5 6 7 8 9 10

For Mama

The strongest woman I know.

Contents

Foreword

By Joel Osteen

I'm so proud of my sister April. She's an amazing communicator and has a great gift to inspire people to reach their potential. Whether your life is going well or you're going through disappointments and things you don't understand, we all want to be better. We want to be a better parent, a better spouse, a better friend, a better encourager, a better coworker, a better boss or manager. God put something deep down inside us that wants to be more like Him, something that keeps pushing us forward and saying, "You weren't born to be average or ordinary; you're meant to increase and rise higher. Don't be satisfied with good enough. You can be better."

Many of us have become conditioned in our minds to thinking we've made too many mistakes, we've reached our limits, we've seen our best days, and we're stuck. But the good news is that you can leave the negative mindsets behind and choose the path that leads to all you were created to be. What God has in front of you is more fulfilling and rewarding than anything you've seen in the past.

My father used to say, "Find your sweet spot," and that is what my youngest sister, April Osteen Simons, has found with her speaking and writing on how you and I can become better. I've seen April face her share of challenges, as we all do, and through it all she encourages us to find ways, both big and small, to make today great, and tomorrow even better.

April's words are filled with encouragement, humor, inspiration, and hope. With the right perspective on what's ahead, and the willingness to open your heart and mind to all that's possible, she shows you how to steer your life toward the positive and press into the next level. I'm encouraged by knowing that the best is yet to come, and that our days and our lives can continually become ***better than ever***.

Introduction

What if I dared to tell you it only takes a few small changes and tweaks to make your life better? Would you be willing to explore that idea? My life is certainly not perfect. I've had my share of challenges, but I can honestly say that, with a bit of extra effort, my life has progressively become better and better.

Life doesn't have to be consistently boring and mundane. We don't have to wait to enjoy it until our kids grow up, or the bank account gets bigger, or even until our waistlines get slimmer. We can make life better today! Our pasts may not have been all that great and our futures may look a bit shaky, but we still have today. And we get to choose what we'll make of it.

Better Than Ever is written from personal experience. It contains real-life stories and practical ways to make anyone's day the best it can be. In this book, we'll explore family, mindsets, and circumstances. Together, we can walk away from settling and make our way to a better future—and laugh a bit along the way!

We're all on a journey to thrive. Being ***better than ever*** is about how we shape our reactions, responses, relationships, and mindset when things aren't going the way we think we'd like for them to go. Life isn't about staying put. It's not about, "Okay, I've grown to this age, so why try anymore?" Life is about making each day better than the day before.

This is my mantra.

Each day, I focus on not allowing the chaos going on around me to override the calm within me. I strive to always look for the good because even in the worst situations, there is good. I want to seek out the positive and express gratitude.

I want every single day to be ***better than ever*** for me, and I want that for you, too. You can change the trajectory of your day, every day, steering it back to the positive and away from the negative. You can use your words to speak life and hope, even when times are difficult. You can stop repeating past behaviors and habits and choose a new, better direction for you and your loved ones. You can cease to embrace ordinary, opting to step out and capture the extraordinary that is waiting for you. Let's make your life's story one worth reading. Let's be ***better than ever***!

—April Osteen Simons

CHAPTER 1

Just Drive

"Action is the foundational key to all success."

—PABLO PICASSO

Many years ago, my kids and I were coming home from a long, crazy day of school followed by basketball games. It was about eight o'clock, way past our normal dinner time, and let me tell you something: my kids were tired and hungry. In fact, they were downright *hangry*! I decided to do what any good modern-day mom would do. I hit the nearest drive-through, so we could hurry home and eat immediately.

We chose a new Mexican food restaurant that we'd all heard was amazing but hadn't had the opportunity to try out. Now let me stop right here and tell you just how much we *love* Mexican food. I honestly believe that it'll be one of the main courses for dinner every night in heaven. The drive-through lane, thankfully, was empty. I pulled up to the first menu board so that everyone could see the choices. After collecting the orders, I crept up to the intercom and rolled down my window. You need to know I have a hard and fast rule. When my window goes down everyone has to be quiet so I can focus. It's also important for you to know that I have to place orders for seven people, including many changes and special requests.

Immediately, everyone got quiet and I gave the first order, then the second. So far, so good, right? Except it was at that precise moment that my kids began to giggle. I raised up my hand, snapped my fingers, and whispered loudly, "Y'all be quiet. I have to focus." (Does anyone else do that?) The kids shifted back into silence. I gave the third order and then the fourth. I felt really good! I remembered all of the orders, got the cheese just right, and the jalapeños were exactly where they needed to be. I was on a roll and pretty proud of myself. Then, after a few moments, a thought occurred to me. *Nobody was talking back to me.*

Just to confirm someone was getting my amazingly perfect order, I looked right into that big intercom and said, "Hey, are you there? Are you getting this?"

Not a sound. I tried once more, "Does anybody hear me?"

As soon as the words came out of my mouth, my kids couldn't contain themselves for another second. They exploded with laughter. My son was literally bowed over backward from laughing so hard. My daughters were rolling in the backseat. I looked at my oldest daughter, Christiana, in the passenger seat, and she had the biggest tears streaming down her face from laughing so hard. I was clueless. I had no idea what my kids had witnessed that was so funny. To be honest, it was making me a little mad!

Finally, I spoke up, in a very serious and loud tone.

"What is going on?"

My son, Garrison, tried to contain himself and leaned over in the front seat. Very loudly, in my right ear, he said, "Mom, you're *talking to a garbage can*!"

Jesus, please take the wheel, and take it from me now. Dear God in heaven, please no. I looked out the car window and there it was, as big as day, a *garbage can*! It was one of those modern, eco-friendly ones with the spout on the top, which I'd mistaken for the intercom speaker. I couldn't believe it. I prayed. *Lord, please don't let anyone be watching from the giant window in the restaurant.*

Well, that was a prayer that I can honestly say went unanswered. I was mortified to be staring at an entire family that was also chuckling at my expense. I was so embarrassed. If that wasn't enough, I looked into my sideview mirror, once again silently seeking God's divine intervention that the drive-through line had remained empty. Another unanswered prayer. Not one, but *five* cars full of people, all laughing. Nobody honked. Nobody tried to save me from embarrassment—not a soul in my car or in any of the other vehicles. *Lord have mercy.*

Looking back, I suppose I should be glad I was able to provide some joy for those people on that particular day. Do you know what I did? I pulled a few feet ahead to the actual intercom with the real person, kept my head down, and gave our order. We picked up the food, pulled into the parking lot, and had a really good laugh together. Truly, we have a memory that will last a lifetime.

I tell you this story because I want you to see a bigger point. I'd gotten so busy "doing stuff" and accomplishing everything that a mom would do (besides talking to a garbage can) that I failed to notice *where I parked my life*. I was sitting in front of a garbage can and talking to it! It probably stank to high heaven and it didn't even faze me. The reality is, all I had to do was pull a few feet ahead to where there was real *life*.

The one thing we all have in common is the fact that *life* happens to everyone. Let's face the truth. It's easy to get overwhelmed with the simple, everyday routine of life. Furthermore, sometimes situations can be just plain hard to decipher. We can easily get the idea that things are passing us by or even running us over! I saw a greeting card that sums it up well. The front stated, "When life gets overwhelming, I've found that a nice long hot bath can solve most of the day's problems." When you open it up, the inside of the card reads, "I've been in here since last Thursday."

The way we start our days can set the standard for what kind of day we'll have. Here are a few good questions we could ask ourselves when we wake up every day:

- Am I parked in front of negativity with a "glass-half-empty" attitude?
- Am I parked in front of defeat, feeling like I'm never going to see victory?
- Am I parked in front of chaos, feeling like everything in my life is in disarray?
- Am I parked in front of stress, tired and worn out, before I even get out of bed?
- Am I parked in front of heartache and disappointment that makes me feel worthless and like I'm never going to get a break?

Whether we realize it or not, where we've parked our lives will greatly impact our outlook. It causes us to see things either negatively or positively. It shapes our days and our attitude. It can affect us emotionally, mentally, and spiritually. Scripture gives us insight. In fact, it shows us we have a choice in how we can live our days. The scripture says, "I have set before you life and death, the blessings and the curses; therefore choose life, that you and your descendants may live." (Deuteronomy 30:19 AMPC) We have both a choice and a vital part to play in how our days will go. We can either choose the negative and focus on everything going wrong or begin to see through eyes of faith and hope and find the good. We can choose to dwell on the problems or on the possibilities. Sometimes all it takes is a simple adjustment in our thinking. It's deciding to "drive" toward life to make our days ***better than ever***.

Mean What You Say

One way to make each day better than the last is through vocal declarations, such as: "No, I'm not staying in this negativity. I'm putting my life in drive and I'm going to position myself where there's an abundance that God has promised me." Or: "My marriage may not be in unity right now, but I'm choosing to park in front of complete restoration." Or: "My kids may not be serving God or living right, but I'm saying, 'As for me and *my* house, we are going to serve the Lord.'"

We may feel completely stressed and overwhelmed, but we can actively choose to station our lives in front of God's perfect peace. When we make these choices, we're setting the standard in our homes. We are driving our families into the life God has designed for them. It starts with us. Brian Tracy said it well: "You are the architect of your own destiny; you are the master of your own fate; you are behind the steering wheel of your life. There are no limitations to what you can do, have, or be. Except the limitations you place on yourself by your own thinking."

I want to encourage you to roll down the window of your life daily and see where you're parked. Is it in the wrong place? Hey! Take it from me. All you have to do is pull up a few feet to where there's life, joy, laughter, fulfillment, peace, and an incredible future! (And maybe even some Mexican food!)

YOUR PURSUIT

Keep moving forward to make your life *better than ever*.

CHAPTER 2

Turn the Page

"You can't start the next chapter of your life if you keep rereading the last one."

—UNKNOWN

My mom and dad were married for forty-four years before he went to heaven in 1999. In fact, if you ask Mama, she'll tell you they were married forty-four years, four months, and six days. They were a great team. Together, they started Lakewood Church in Houston, Texas. They had very humble beginnings, literally starting the church in a feed store.

A place that had previously been used to feed chickens was eventually used to feed followers God's messages of faith, hope, and love. The small church had only room for 234 people. Through faith, patience, and years of hard work, the church exploded to over twenty-thousand-plus members and a television ministry that continues to bless and minister to people around the world. Mama and Daddy had a heart for people—for the hurting, the sick, and the lonely. Throughout my life, I watched as they loved on, prayed for, and gave hope to those who walked through the doors of Lakewood Church. I know they didn't do it because they had to. They started the church, nurtured it, and fought for its success because they were passionate about seeing lives transformed by the grace of God.

I'm blessed to have grown up in a home where all of us kids were taught that every single life is important to God and that everyone deserves another chance. Fast forward many years to when my dad was promoted to heaven. He left behind kids, grandkids, and of course, my mom. She was twelve years younger than Daddy, so she was only in her mid-sixties when he died. Mama still had plenty of life ahead of her, and it was interesting to see the turn her life would take.

Sure, she missed Daddy greatly, but she realized his departure from this earth didn't mean her life—nor God's plan for her life—was over. Her strength, through our family's loss, taught us all that life really does go on. With one dream dead, God provided Mama with eyes to see that He would be faithful and provide a new dream to keep her busy and happy. In essence, a new chapter that had yet to be written was presented to her. She grabbed it and dove in headfirst. She knew she had more to give, and she was eager to do just that.

I watched as my little five-foot-two-inch, one-hundred-pound mama put her new, AD (after daddy) life into a gear I never knew she had. Not just a second gear, but a second, third, and fourth gear as well. Mama decided to turn the page. Instead of shrinking back and fading into the background after she lost her life partner, I watched in awe as Mama stepped up her game and rose to a whole new level. She studied the plate of what life had thrown at her and became a key player in her own right.

For my entire life, I had a front-row seat to witness Mama's ability to give of herself, and it was clear, immediately, that this new chapter would be no different. She instinctively knew that it wasn't time for her to retreat into isolation, but quite the opposite. She had to keep going. After all, it's not about how you start, it's how you finish. Mama has lived by that saying her entire life, knowing full well, and especially after Daddy died, that we aren't guaranteed even one second of time on this earth. It's been twenty-plus years now, and Mama has hardly slowed down.

Mama is the biggest lover of people I've ever seen in my life. She still takes time for each and every person who either approaches her or who she decides could use some nurturing attention. She values and speaks life into every one of them. If you need prayer, you come to Mama. She's going to pray for you like nobody's business. You're going to leave knowing that you've been prayed over completely. That's for sure. She stood by and supported the transition of the church to my older brother. And you better believe she's there at every single service, supporting him (and correcting his grammar) every step of the way.

Even today, Mama still travels regularly and shares her miracle story of being healed of cancer. (I'll talk more about Mama's cancer-beating journey later.) She knows God gave her that miracle, not just for her sake, but to give hope and life to those in need of their own miracle.

How are you choosing to live your life? Did you know that the decision to live actively, outwardly in the world actually starts with an inward decision? We can decide to keep going and not wall ourselves in, or throw up giant boundaries of protection and isolate ourselves. It's reminding ourselves daily that even when the worst has happened, we will, more likely than not, be blessed with more days ahead. We can believe that means more opportunities for each day to be ***better than ever***.

I know it might be extremely difficult, but I'm praying that when you feel like you're drowning in life, you'll make the decision to not stop swimming, even if it means dog-paddling until you catch your breath and can manage a better stroke. When you think no one in this world cares about you, I'm hoping you'll remember that not only does God care about you, but the scripture tells us, "The Lord is close to the brokenhearted; he rescues those whose spirits are crushed."

(Psalm 34:18 NLT) Without doubt, He won't abandon you or walk out of your life. He will never stop loving you. Turn the page.

You can't change what happened. The only thing you can do is keep moving forward. When something has ended, that doesn't mean God won't have a new chapter with your name on it, waiting for you to dive in and start writing. You may think you've already lived your best days. Oh, let me tell you, you haven't. Your best days are right now. Get a new dream. God isn't finished with your story yet.

Dream at Every Age

When Mama was seventy-eight years old, (did you get that? Seventy-eight!) twelve years after Daddy passed away, she had a new dream. She told me she was going to create a drive-through healing service! (Something is definitely going on with me and my family and drive-through situations!) When she told me her idea, I have to say, I had no clue what she was talking about.

"You know, some people are so sick, they don't have the strength to come into the church and sit through a service and wait for prayer," Mama explained. "Even the car ride is too much for some of them. So I'm going to stand out in the circular drive in front of the church, and people can come from hospitals, in ambulances, and from their homes, and when they pull through, I'm going to get in their car and pray for them and give hope to their weary bodies."

She had a vision of exactly what she wanted to make happen and she was determined to carry it out. A few weeks later, Mama had her first drive-through healing service. She opened doors of ambulances and cars and just crawled inside and breathed life into people who were desperate to receive it. Many had been given up on by the doctors, something Mama was well familiar with. She was passionate about these people, and her prayers demonstrated that passion. She counted it an honor to be able to pray for those who were so sick and in varying states of need. That was only the first of many drive-through ministry events that Mama has had. And as long as Mama has her way, I'm sure there'll be many more.

Please don't stop because you believe you've seen a dream die, a relationship end, or maybe a loved one pass. Please don't stop if you've endured financial hardship, or a stalled-out career. Despite the magnitude of *any* situation, don't throw in the towel. Trust God and remind yourself that He is the God of promises. Those promises will comfort you. Maybe you're all alone and don't feel like life is worth living. You're not and it is! Don't quit! Your life matters and things will get better, if you can only ride out this current storm. Remember that with God, your life can be ***better than ever***.

I'm reminded of the story of a pastor at a church named Almighty God Baptist Church. He was working late on a Friday when he decided to call his wife to tell her he'd be home later than expected. He called from his office phone, but when he dialed their number, the phone rang and rang. No one ever answered. He thought it was strange because he knew she was home. He hung up and, a few minutes later, tried again. After the first ring, she answered. He asked why she didn't answer the phone when he'd called previously. She told him the telephone never rang. They didn't think any more about it and went about their evening.

The next Monday, the preacher went back to his office at Almighty God Church. He was sitting at his desk when the phone rang. The person on the other end wanted to know why he'd received a phone call on Friday night.

"The phone rang and rang," the man admitted, "but I didn't answer."

The preacher realized he must have called the wrong number. He explained and apologized for calling so late.

"No worry," the man replied, "but let me tell you my story. I was going to commit suicide that night. I cried out to God and said, 'God, if you're real and you don't want me to do this, I need you now.'"

The man continued, "At that very moment, you called me. On the caller ID it said, 'Almighty God.' I looked at it and I was too afraid to answer."

Let me tell you something. There is never a place where you are and God's not. If you're struggling with whether or not God needs you, the answer is yes. If you're wondering if your life matters, the answer is a resounding, emphatic *yes*. If you're questioning whether there's more up ahead in store for you, the answer is *absolutely*. No matter how old or how young you are, no matter what you've gone through or are currently facing, God isn't finished with you yet.

I pray you decide today that you'll take a step of faith and move out of whatever discouragement and disappointment you might feel trapped in. Open up the curtains. Let the sunshine in. Get dressed, put one foot in front of the other, and keep on living. You can do it. Turn the page. It's time for the next chapter to begin.

YOUR PURSUIT

Understand, remember, and accept that *you matter*. Open your heart and mind to what God wants for you in the coming days and transform your life to become *better than ever*.

CHAPTER 3

Find Your Wag

"The two most important days in your life are the day you were born and the day you find out why!"

—MARK TWAIN

When our beautiful little Yorkie named Missy was just a puppy, I noticed something different about her. Every time I came home, she and our slightly older dog, Trevor, met me at the door. Now, Trevor was always so happy to see me. His enjoyment at something so trivial as my arrival home would always melt my heart. He'd bark, wag his tail, and jump up on me, wanting every drop of my attention. Missy, on the other hand, would follow Trevor to the door and stare at me with her cute face twisted into a puzzled look. She simply stood there, no hint that she was at all happy that I'd made it home. Honestly, I felt bad. It seemed like something was wrong with Missy. I didn't tell anyone, but I was extremely concerned.

As time passed, I continued to notice Missy's behavior, especially compared to Trevor's. Missy never barked. She never jumped up on me. And, as if that wasn't bad enough, I never saw her wag her tail! I truly pondered how that was even possible. In my estimation, when a dog wags their tail, it means *happy*! (Okay, don't tell me if I'm wrong.)

It actually made my heart hurt to think that our precious little Missy wasn't happy in our home. I was on a mission. I was bound and determined to see our pup joyful. Every time I walked through the door, I watched for Missy to show me any sign of happiness. I watched for her to wag her tail. I had no idea how long I'd be watching, but it was one month, two months, six months, and then... finally something happened. After nine long, unhappy, non-wagging months, Missy Lou Simons met me at the door and her tiny, stubby tail was wagging like crazy! I can't even begin to tell you how exhilarated I was. To this day, I have no idea what happened or what changed. I do know, without a doubt, that my little Missy had her own personal breakthrough! Missy finally seemed content. Every time I came home, from that point forward, she greeted me with the cutest little tail swish you've ever seen. I even think she smiled, too.

Okay, you're probably thinking, what in the world does Missy and her tail wagging (or not wagging) have to do with me? I'm glad you asked. This is really deep. You might want to sit down. Are you ready?

Missy found her wag!

I'm 100 percent convinced that's what happened. And guess what? You, my friend, need to find your wag as well! What do I mean by this statement? Allow me to explain by asking you a series of questions:

- What excites you?
- What's important to you?
- What makes you feel alive?
- What lights you up as you hear someone talking about it?

I'm not just talking about your work or how you make a living. I'm talking about the underneath stuff, the real you, the person who just might be buried under the stress and pressures of life. Let's be honest. Stuff happens. It's easy for our zeal to get buried, stuck on the back shelf, or even worse, to be abandoned all together. At various times, the things we go through cause feelings of worthlessness and failure. These attitudes and emotions can come from how we respond to our past, parenthood struggles, health issues, work situations, paralyzing debt, and so on. Whatever the circumstance might be, life has the potential to overwhelm us all. During these instances, we can easily lose our place, our focus, and our grounding.

Turning a Negative Situation into Good

A close friend of mine went through a divorce. She left a very abusive situation. That alone would qualify her as an amazing, strong woman, but she also raised two kids, worked full time and, believe it or not, somehow managed to carve out space enough to go to school until she earned a master's degree in business. You'd think this woman certainly wouldn't lack for confidence. At least, that's what I thought—until she told me this story.

One day, she was watching my mom and me on television. She heard my mom tell the story of how my dad had gone through a divorce before he married my mom. My friend began to listen closely. Mama explained how Daddy—even though he felt like a failure because his marriage didn't work out—discovered God didn't hold his mistakes against him. In fact, He still had an amazing plan for his life. A few years later, he met my mom, and they tied the knot and had five kids. (I hear the youngest one is just incredible...haha.) He then went on to build Lakewood Church in Houston, Texas. My parents pastored together for more than forty years until he went to Heaven in 1999. My friend told me that their story suddenly opened her mind to new possibilities. She had an epiphany of God's amazing grace and unconditional love. "God can still use me, even though I've gone through some terrible things," she declared. My friend realized the bad things that had happened couldn't define or limit her. She was sure that God *still* had an amazing plan for her life. In fact, God used what she went through to propel her into helping people around the world who were going through similar situations.

I never would've guessed that my confident, smart, amazing friend ever felt self-doubt and regret. I thank God that my friend got her wag back.

We have to realize that the enemy wants to keep us buried underneath our mistakes. He wants to magnify our failures to the point where we feel inadequate. He wants to steal our purposes and keep us in shame. When we recognize the lies of the enemy and choose *not* to listen and begin to walk in the grace and forgiveness of Jesus, we become a force to be reckoned with!

Your story, just like my friend's, can be used to help pull someone through a difficult situation to become ***better than ever***. What the enemy means for evil, God will turn around for good. Your story is important. Don't forget that. Don't try to erase it or hide from it. Forgiveness is true, complete, and for everyone. Your story isn't there to highlight your imperfections and failures, but instead to bring hope, healing, and life to people in a way that only you can demonstrate. Remember, your past doesn't determine your future—God does. Whether you have to deal with fear, not feeling capable or talented enough, or just being tired, let me encourage you today to dig deep. People you don't even know yet need what you have to offer. God has given you special and unique talents that His world needs. Take back your zeal for life. Repossess your hope. Plant that smile back on your beautiful face. Get your happy back. When you wake every morning, sit up and tell the world, "I have a reason for getting out of bed! I'm excited for this day!"

Before you know it, you'll be just like that old joke about playing a country music song backwards: you'll get your house back, your dog back, your truck back, your wife back, and your hair back, too. Okay, maybe not all of these examples apply, but you get the idea! Don't let your passion and purpose lie dormant. Don't let the dreams and talents God has given you go to waste. You're not past your prime. You're not too old or too young. You haven't failed too many times. Let me assure you, if you're still breathing, you still have purpose. Listen, if Missy can find her wag, then there is no question you can too. You have what it takes. Get that wag back and start living life to the fullest. Remember, more than you can or possibly will ever know, the world needs what you have to offer. When you go for it and live as God intended, you'll realize that you're destined to get out there and wag...and forever strive to be ***better than ever***.

YOUR PURSUIT

Do what makes you happy so each day can become *better than ever*.

CHAPTER 4

Own the Dash

"In the middle of every difficulty lies opportunity."

—ALBERT EINSTEIN

Have you ever thought about what makes an Oreo cookie so good? When you get right down to it, it's the yummy cream in the middle that sets this cookie apart. And I'm not even talking about Double Stuf (I looked it up to check, and yes, it's spelled with one *F*)—the original Oreo cookie will do. I mean, come on...I'm starting to get hungry just writing about those cream-filled treats! (Trust me, I'm going somewhere with this.)

Now, imagine if an Oreo didn't have the filling. You'd just have two, plain, dry, boring, round cookies. Nothing to write home about and certainly nothing special. It's what's in the middle that makes an Oreo cookie an *Oreo Cookie*! And it's probably the reason why billions have been sold since they were created. What's in the middle *really* matters. Now, think about the trajectory of the human journey for a minute. Isn't it similar to our cookie? Isn't it about what happens in the middle—in between the dashes (just like this)—that makes our lives valuable?

Everyone's dash is unique and different. When I bring home those Oreos, some of my kids eat them right out of the bag. Others will twist the chocolate sides apart and immediately lick that yummy filling. And then there's my son, who takes a cookie and dips the entire thing into a huge glass of milk. Hey, you can tell a lot about a person by the way they eat an Oreo! In a similar fashion, those precious moments that splash down in between the landmark events of our lives actually show us who we are and what we're made of. The in-between times say much more about us than maybe even the epic moments do. The middle is definitely where the "stuff" (or should I say the "Stuf") of life happens—where we discover our resilience.

In-between times are where:

- we're going from point **A** to point **B**,
- we're caught between a rock and a hard place,
- we're in that "waiting place,"
- we're waiting for our breakthrough,
- we're waiting for our miracle,
- we're waiting for things to get better,
- we're waiting for things to change.

In other words, we're waiting for the next season. It's not unusual to think that all of us are alternately coming in and going out of the in-between spaces of our lives almost every day. Those times are what make the journey. They're the very moments that get us to where we're destined to be.

The way a person handles the in-between places says a lot. It's during the waiting that we tend to find out the good, the bad, and the ugly about ourselves. In essence, we discover our own inner composition, what we truly believe, and the depth of our faith.

The in-between times are where the rubber meets the road, especially when it comes to our spiritual walk. God has an amazing future in store for all of us. But we must also remember that the enemy is equally committed to his plan for our lives. That's right. The enemy has a mission as well, and he's fully dedicated to keeping us all from the gifts God has in store for us. The enemy doesn't want us to have what God has promised we'll have, or do what God says we can do, or even accomplish the things He has put on our hearts. God wants us to move forward. But the enemy prefers us stuck, spinning our wheels, or even better, moving backward and further away from God. God wants to *give* us life. The enemy wants to drain our lives. God wants us to succeed, while the enemy would love to see us fail.

Make no mistake. There is an epic battle being fought daily over how our stories will end. It's nothing short of our destinies that Satan wants to keep us from stepping into. His greatest fear is our tomorrows. We can look back at scripture and read how Satan tried to kill Moses as a baby and Joseph as a teenager. At that time in either of their lives, they hadn't yet accomplished much, but both men were destined to do great things. Satan's plan is always to try and take us out before we can reach our God-purposed destinies. The enemy also tried to take Jesus out as a baby. As a baby, He hadn't yet healed the sick or caused the lame to walk. But Satan knew what was coming. He figured if he could take Jesus out as an infant, He would never make it to the cross, or be resurrected and redeem mankind for all of eternity.

Trust God in All Seasons

Scripture continually warns us to be aware of the strategies of the enemy. Don't be caught off guard. Be sober, alert, and cautious at all times. "That enemy of yours, the devil, prowls around like a roaring lion, seeking someone to devour." (1 Peter 5:8 AMP) The enemy will try to pull us off course completely or cause us to be distracted and frustrated about our "today" so that we'll be too worn out to make it to our tomorrow, much less the amazing future that God has in store for us. The enemy wants to wear us down with the "stuff" of life with just about as much energy and vigor as God uses to grow us. Where Satan wants to steal our joy and overwhelm us with life, God wants to extend our faith and see us thrive, regardless of our circumstances. The enemy would like for us to question if the promises of God are even true, and then to be filled with corresponding doubt and worry. Yet our Savior, Jesus, wants to lift us up as He reassures us that "this too shall pass." He wants us to know that great things are surely in store for those who love Him.

And this is the good news. God has great things in store for us! He wants our days to be ***better than ever***, even though we may not see it or feel it. He's constantly working behind the scenes on our behalves. Scripture tells us: "For it is God who is all the while effectually at work in you..." (Philippians 2:13 AMPC) God is all the while working. He is lining up solutions. He's setting things up behind the scenes. He's getting things ready. There's no doubt He knows about everything we're going through. He's already prepared a way out.

It's important to understand that, just because we don't see anything happening, that doesn't imply that God isn't working on our behalves. Sometimes, we're left wondering when God is going to move; all the while, God is left wondering when we're going to slow down to wait on His perfect timing. We don't know what God is up to. He is doing things according to His plans and His timing. Will you trust Him in seasons of silence? Will you keep the faith, even when you don't see anything happening? Will you commit to fighting through the in-between times? One verse in the Bible reads, "Let us not get tired of doing what is right, for after a while we will reap a harvest of blessing if we don't get discouraged and give up." (Galatians 6:9 TLB)

In the Bible, Joseph waited for thirteen years. Abraham waited for twenty-five years. Moses waited for forty years, and Jesus waited thirty. They *all* had to trust God during the difficult seasons of life.

They had to trust Him when they saw nothing. They had to stand in faith when they were given a promise, but had to wait years, and sometimes even decades, to see those promises come to pass. They still lived their in-betweens well.

Waiting is where our character comes to the surface. It's where we find out if we really believe what we say we believe enough to live it out. The in-between times are a place for growing. They are opportunities to improve—and to become stronger.

Remember, It's Not Just About You

One day you'll look back and see how far you have come and how much you've grown. It's also important to remember that these times aren't just about you. While you're waiting, you're teaching your children how to act and believe during difficult times. You're teaching them by example what to do when tough circumstances arise. You're showing them what you believe about God when the "stuff" of life hits you squarely in the face. Every time you don't give up, you're teaching your children to not give up when something gets hard. Every time you get back up after falling down, you're teaching your children to be "get back uppers." Every time you speak life during difficulty, you're teaching your children to speak life. Every time you show your children you still love God and believe in Him during a challenge, you're teaching your children to run *to* God and not away from Him.

Wait well. People will remember how you walk through the in-betweens of life. God will never leave you during the waiting. The scripture assures us that "God is our refuge and strength, an ever-present help in trouble." (Psalm 46:1 NIV) Keep the faith. And remember, no storm lasts forever. The page will turn. A new chapter will begin. God is working as you're waiting. Live the dash well. It's the part that matters. It's the good stuff...the God stuff that makes every day ***better than ever***.

YOUR PURSUIT

Embrace the times in between the dash—
the times when you're waiting for something to happen—
to make life *better than ever*.

CHAPTER 5

Find the Joy

"Of all the attitudes we can acquire, surely the attitude of gratitude is the most important and by far the most life-changing."

—ZIG ZIGLAR

In February of last year, I began to have trouble with my left leg. I'm an avid walker. I usually get in anywhere from five to ten miles a day when I'm in town. I love it. The cadence clears my mind and I can definitely accomplish some of my best thinking. Even though the pain didn't keep me from moving, it did restrict the distance I was able to walk. Well, at first that was the case. Then, after about two weeks, the pain increased to a level I didn't even realize I could experience. I suddenly found myself in such horrendous agony that I could barely take a few steps without having to sit down. I sought relief by first fulfilling my due-diligence obligations with visits to both my regular doctor as well as a chiropractor. Needless to say, I was finding no solution and the pain was getting worse.

After several attempts at using a variety of pain relief medications that didn't relieve my pain one bit, my doctor sent me to get an MRI. I was hoping this would provide answers, but unfortunately, that was not the case. We still had no idea where the searing pain was coming from. I just couldn't find relief anywhere. Things had gotten so bad that I had to begin canceling speaking engagements, and that, my friends, was almost as painful as the leg. Missing an engagement was not something I'd ever done before. I felt terrible about it.

Almost as a last-ditch effort, my primary doctor referred me to three different specialists. She provided me phone numbers (and some hopeful optimism) as she sent me away to continue trying to solve the riddle. Using the most scientific method I could dredge up from the depths of my soul, I randomly picked one of the three numbers provided. Hey, you gotta start somewhere, right? I gave the first office a call. Miraculously, I happened to connect with one of the top neurosurgeons in Texas. This was truly amazing because he was completely booked for months in advance, but he just happened to have an appointment available. I took it.

By the time we met in his office, he had intricately reviewed my MRI, and I could immediately tell he was concerned. He said the culprit for my intense, indescribable pain was sciatica, which I believe is straight from the pit of Hades. The doctor insisted with great urgency that he be allowed to operate, not only to alleviate the trauma happening in my spine, but also to prevent permanent nerve damage in my leg. I was immediately concerned as well! This top doctor actually rearranged his schedule to make me the first patient for surgery on the following Monday. When he said urgent, he wasn't kidding around. Talk about a blessing within a string of blessings! The thought of experiencing relief from my pain was wonderfully exciting to me. As far as I was concerned, Monday couldn't come soon enough.

On the day of surgery, the pain was so excruciating that I'm not kidding when I say I literally couldn't walk. Sciatica is, by far, the worst pain I have ever experienced in my life...and y'all, I have had five kids, two without epidurals. Enough said! (And all the moms will say, "Amen!") I went into surgery in unbearable pain and, I'm thrilled to say that, a few hours later, I walked out of that hospital on my own. Did you get that? I *walked* out! Let me tell you something—there is a God and He loves me (haha). I continue to thank God for the amazing team that worked on me. I can't express how grateful I am to be on the other side of that never-ending pain and for the gift of being able to walk pain-free once again. Every single day, I tell God how grateful I am.

I think about my gratitude when I'm walking my route and each time I reach down to scoop up my wonderful grand babies. I'm overwhelmed with a core-level sense of gratitude. When I see others struggling to walk or acting as if they're in pain, I'm reminded of the miracle of being pain-free that He gifted to me. I also say a prayer for these other people because I remember what it was like to be in that position—to be so pain ridden that basic tasks were nearly impossible to accomplish.

The God Things

Yes, I tell God thank you often, but I'm pretty certain He never gets tired of hearing it. In scripture, Paul shares, "In everything give thanks; for this is the will of God in Christ Jesus for you." (1 Thessalonians 5:18 NKJV) There's something about being grateful that changes our world. It shifts our mindset. We begin to notice the little things happening in our lives. I call them the God things. The act of being grateful opens our eyes to what we have, as opposed to steering our focus onto what we lack. Not only that, remember that gratefulness is also good for the body. That's right, experiencing gratitude is actually beneficial to your overall health. Gratitude allows better sleep. We're more able to attack the day with positivity and energy. When we have a lifestyle of gratitude, we carry less anxiety and stress and more vitality. Isn't that exciting? Gratitude helps us to become more peaceful. Hey, who doesn't want that?

However, focusing on gratitude is a choice. Alphonse Karr said, "Some people grumble because roses have thorns; I am thankful that the thorns have roses." I love that. Gratitude changes our perspective. It helps us to look on the bright side of life. Take my mom, for example. She has two lists. One is her concern list and the other is her grateful list. Whenever she has something heavy on her heart, she writes it down on the concern list. Then, she simply gives the items on it to God and she thanks Him for taking it. There is no big religious prayer that she performs. She simply talks to God like she has a relationship with Him, which, of course, she does. When her prayer is answered, she goes back to her concern list and crosses it off, and then moves it over to her grateful list.

How many times does God give us miracles along the way? Sometimes, we focus so intently on waiting for the ginormous miracle that we forget to thank God for all the little answers to our prayers that He has provided along the way. When we can look back at all the things that have gone right in our lives, it shifts our vision away from our present problems. If we do a little reflecting, we just might discover our world isn't as bad as our minds may be trying to tell us it is. In fact, we might see that it's really pretty good.

If you think about it, there are so many reasons to be grateful in life. How about being grateful for having food on the table? Or for a paycheck? Hey, it may not be what you want, but at least you have one. How about your kids...you know, the ones that are driving you crazy...the ones God said are a blessing in your life? You can even be grateful for being able to pay your rent and having a roof over your head. And there's always the amazing gift of today. You may not be where you want to be, but thank God you're not where you used to be!

Be grateful for the problems you don't have, and for the pain that isn't there. Be grateful you're not in the hospital, living on the streets, or in prison. Some people aren't afforded the same blessings. Shift your perspective.

An elderly man named George, who was well into his eighties, had a routine he followed. Every day, at 9:15 a.m. on the dot, he went to the nursing home to have breakfast with his beautiful wife. She suffered from Alzheimer's and hadn't recognized him for the past five years. A nurse in the facility watched as George came every single day, happy and excited to see his wife. She saw him feed her and make conversation with her, even though she never replied. It didn't seem to matter to George. The nurse noted his gentleness, and how he wiped his wife's face after he finished feeding her.

Finally, one day, she stopped him as he came into the facility. She said, "George, why do you show up every single day at 9:15 a.m. to have breakfast with your wife when it's clear that she no longer knows who you are?"

George smiled, patted the nurse on the hand and responded, "She may no longer know who I am, but I still know who she is."

George is someone who has shifted his perspective. I love how he didn't focus on their time apart, or on what he was getting in return, but instead chose to focus on what they had together. He didn't dwell on the fact that she didn't know who he was, but instead, put all his attention on the woman he still loved with all of his heart. I know it's easy to focus on the losses, but I encourage you to be thankful for what you still have. Turn your thoughts toward gratitude. I've found that writing down what I'm grateful for is so rewarding. Most every day I write down at least one thing that brings joy to my life. I want you to consider doing the same. Allow me to show you what I'm talking about. Here are some of the things I'm grateful for:

Early morning, a warm blanket, coffee, and my Bible.
A clean house.
A clean car.
Warm, homemade chocolate cake.
The right pair of shoes. (I know, you might have expected this to be higher on the list… Ha ha!)

Christmas.
The perfect pair of boots.
Warm fuzzy socks.
A full tank of gas.
Red velvet cupcakes from Sprinkles bakery.
Yummy-smelling candles.
Hot bubble baths.
Turkey chili and Fritos on a cold, winter day.
Passing a cop who's hiding while I'm totally going the speed limit.
My grand babies.
Listening to Frank Sinatra.
Shopping.
My Keurig coffee maker.
Paying for the person behind me, without them knowing.
Red Christmas cups at Starbucks.
The sound of rain.
The sound of my kids laughing.
Remembering the sound of my father's voice.
Living in a free country.
Seeing lives changed.
Waking up.
Breathing.
Getting another chance to see another day.

Joy and happiness aren't always found in the extraordinary. They're sprinkled all over your life. They include celebrating and being grateful for what God has already given you right now, right here, all around you. Every day, every breath is a gift. You were given today while some people weren't given that opportunity. Do what you can with the time you have right now. Cultivate a mindset of gratitude and watch your life become ***better than ever***. Look for the small miracles along the way. Be mindful of the things so many people take for granted. Life doesn't have to get good for you to start enjoying it. Start and end each day with a grateful heart. And just you watch. The moment you start acting like life is a blessing is the moment it starts to become one.

YOUR PURSUIT

Make the active choice to acknowledge your blessings and give words of gratitude to God. When you stop to notice and appreciate all that you have, from the very simple to the very grand, your life becomes filled with moments that are *better than ever*.

CHAPTER 6

Adjust Your Focus

"Where focus goes, energy flows."

—TONY ROBBINS

A few years ago, I was on a plane traveling from London to Dallas. Understand, this is not a short flight. In fact, it's listed as 4,747.38 miles, with a flying time of about nine hours. Eight hours and forty minutes were pretty much routine. The captain came over the intercom system and informed us that we would be landing in twenty-five minutes. As you might imagine, we were all more than ready to get our feet onto solid ground, and many of us were happy to get back home. I was thankful that the flight had been completely uneventful, without even a trace of turbulence. You know, the way it's supposed to be! Well, this wouldn't be a story worth telling if everything went perfectly. Things were about to change, and change they did, in a big ol', Texas-sized way.

Five minutes hadn't passed when, all of a sudden, our ride was massively bumpy. Then, without warning, the angle of the plane executed into a considerable drop. I don't know how much it actually fell, but it was enough to make our stomachs roll. It felt like we were on a giant roller coaster, where the plunge is scary and a little fun, all at the same time. We looked at each other and began to laugh, all the while holding onto the armrest a little bit tighter. I had no idea what was coming just around the bend. You see, moments later, our once perfectly calm flight demonstrated yet another drop...and then another. The last one made the previous one feel like tiny speed bumps almost too small to even mention. The drink my daughter was holding flew up into the air and over the seat, landing squarely in my lap. I definitely wasn't laughing anymore. And neither was anyone else.

I distinctly remember looking up after the third incident to see what the flight attendants were doing. I reasoned if they're calm and carrying on with a "business as usual" attitude, then everything must be okay. Well, so much for that. I saw the flight attendants scurrying to the nearest empty seats where they quickly strapped themselves in. Okay, not what I needed or wanted to see. *Next time I'll keep my head down.* Then, I did what any good Christian does when she sees her life flash before her eyes. I started praying. I think it's safe to say, my prayer life took on a whole new level.

God, if you're really there...God, I have kids at home who need me...I'm too young to die. I was quoting scriptures, asking for forgiveness, singing hymns in my head.... I think I even got re-saved! If there had been a glass water in front of me, I probably would have re-baptized myself. Hey, don't judge me! I was desperate and giving it my all.

Obviously, we made it back. The third plunge through the air marked the end of the excitement on the flight from Hades, I mean London. I'm sure those last-minute prayers of mine really were the thing that pulled us through the whole ordeal. I was never so glad to see the ground in all of my life.

Not long after my "near-death experience," I was thinking about everything that'd happened. How close were we really? How much trouble were we in? Was my life actually going to be cut short? And which one of those deeply spiritual, end-of-life prayers had actually saved us? Then all of sudden, I realized something important. I'd focused so much on the deadly twenty minutes of turbulence that I failed to see that, in all actuality, we had also experienced eight hours and forty minutes of absolute peace and calm.

Think about this. Eight hours and forty minutes of *total peace* without a single ounce of worry. And yet, my conversations in the days and weeks following centered around twenty minutes of turbulence. My response showed me how easy it is to lose sight of everything that's going *right* in our lives and how we can choose, instead, to focus on everything that's going *wrong*. If we're not careful, we can completely overlook how far God has brought us and how faithful He has already been. The distractions of life can steal our focus. The challenges we're facing can cause us to dwell on the difficulties alone. But that's only part of the story!

Here's how it happens:

- First, we become distracted by an incident, which begins the process of stealing our focus.
- Next, what we now focus on (the incident) becomes magnified in our minds.
- Then, what we're thinking about burrows down deep into our hearts.
- And finally, what's nestled in our hearts starts to come out of our mouths and shapes our environment.

The reality is, no matter how bad things are, you can always find ways to make them worse. In these moments, we have to resist the enemy and readjust our focus. Our focus can truly make or break us. It can set us up or set us back. It can encourage or discourage. What we choose to focus on naturally is going to become bigger, so it's up to us to specify where we'll aim the lens.

Where will you aim your lens? Zig Ziglar once said, "When you focus on problems, you get more problems. When you focus on possibilities, you have more opportunities." How can you change your focus?

Here are a few suggestions:

- Focus on what you have, instead of what you're missing.
- Focus on how it *can* be done, instead of why it won't be done.
- Focus on moving forward, instead of being stuck.
- Focus on getting back up again, instead of all the reasons you're down.
- Focus on your strengths, instead of your weaknesses.

In other words, instead of dwelling on how far you have to go, *focus* on how far you've come!

We really have to guard our focus like our life depends on it, because to some degree it does. The scripture lays it out very clearly by telling us what to focus on: "Whatever is true, whatever is noble, whatever is right, whatever is pure, whatever is lovely, whatever is admirable—if anything is excellent or praiseworthy—think about such things." (Philippians 4:8 NIV) Another Bible translation says we should center our thoughts on "the best, not the worst; the beautiful, not the ugly; things to praise, not to curse." (Philippians 4:8–9 MSG)

How Our Focus Blesses Others

When I was taking steps to prepare for back surgery, I met with several specialists for various tests. The one that I remember vividly was designed to measure the nerve function in my leg. This was accomplished by the doctor hooking me up to all kinds of contraptions, and then graduating to the not-so-pleasant procedure of pricking my legs with needles. It was very uncomfortable and painful.

To get my mind off of my predicament and shift my focus from me to something else, I started up a conversation with my doctor.

I complimented her skin because it was flawless. She had her hair tucked under a scarf, so her complexion was especially visible. She stopped what she was doing and looked at me as if in disbelief.

"Really?" she asked.

"You have such a beautiful glow," I responded.

The doctor laughed. "It must be the chemo."

She went on to tell me she had just finished up her eighth round of chemotherapy a few days prior. I couldn't believe it. She looked so healthy. She went on to say that she had been diagnosed with stage four cancer and that this was her second bout with the deadly disease. Turns out she used the scarf to hide her hair loss. Almost at a loss for words, I told her I would've never known.

"Thank you," she said, assuring me that her present condition was "because of a lot of prayers."

As she continued the procedure, I debated as to whether or not I should say anything else, but the fact that she mentioned prayer led me to tell her that I'd seen a miracle in someone who'd been given up on by doctors.

"My mom went through a battle with cancer and was given just a few weeks to live, but through faith and prayer, she made it through and continued to live a healthy, cancer-free life, all these years later," I explained.

The doctor's face lit up and her eyes got big. She could hardly wait to get the words out: "You are one of two people who has ever heard my situation and offered me hope. Most people tell me about all the people that they know who had received the same diagnosis and the stories usually end with them telling me how this or that person died. But not you."

Her eyes became glassy as she continued. "In fact, the other lady who gave me hope even brought me a book about someone who was healed of cancer. It has scriptures all throughout the book that I try to read most every day. It's been my lifeline. It's a book by Dodie Osteen."

At that moment, I no longer noticed the pain from the needles. My focus had definitely shifted, and I no longer felt bothered by the sciatica that'd been draining the life out of me.

"Dodie Osteen is my mother," I said.

The doctor began to cry. I realized this was a divine moment, orchestrated by God. Out of all the billions of people in the world, God had intricately woven our paths together inside a hospital, in the midst of our pain and suffering, so that hope and life could be exchanged. Wow! This still gives me goosebumps. We serve an awesome God!

I just love how God works. I think He's often trying to show us that there are people all around who are fighting battles that are so much worse than what we're facing. We have to adjust our focus to see it, and when we do, we can spread His love and kindness to help others. In situations that seem to us to be our worst, there's always someone who would love to trade places. I like this quote by Denzel Washington: "At the end of the day, it's not about what you have or even what you've accomplished…it's about who you've lifted up, who you've made better. It's about what you've given back."

When we focus on what we have, we see the good in our lives and in others' lives. And when we see the good, we can pass it along to others. Some people don't have anyone to help them when they're down. They don't have anyone to speak an encouraging word of hope over their lives. They don't have anyone helping them readjust their focus. Have you ever thought that *you* might be the one person who can make a remarkable difference in someone else's life? You might be the individual who can infuse them with hope in the middle of what may be, in their eyes, a hopeless situation.

You might be *the* person creating *the* moment that helps someone shift their focus. And in the process, you could be helping someone else become ***better than ever***.

What You Focus on Flourishes

A professor decided to give his students a pop quiz. He handed out the exams with the text facing down and then asked the students to turn the papers over. To everyone's surprise, there were no questions on the quiz. Oddly enough, there was only a singular black dot in the center of the paper. The professor told the students to write about what they saw on the paper. You could see the looks of confusion on the student's faces as they hesitantly started the surprising task. After everyone had turned in the tests, the professor began reading each student's answers aloud. All of them defined the black dot and tried to explain its position on the paper. After he read all of the quizzes, he told the kids he wasn't going to grade the assignment, but he wanted them to realize that every single one of them focused on the black dot. Not one talked about the white part of the paper. At this point, he now had every student's undivided attention. He went on to share with the students that it's easy in life to solely focus on the bad things that are happening to us or around us—money problems, relationship challenges, health issues, disappointments in life—which are the dark spots. He stressed how these black dots are so small in comparison to everything else we have in our lives, yet most choose to allow those black dots to fill and pollute their minds. He encouraged the students to take their eyes off of the black dots and enjoy the blessings and moments they were a part of while here on this earth. He wished for them to be happy and live a life filled with joy and love.

What an amazing lesson to be learned. Not just for those students, but for all of us. What we see really does matter. Maybe it's time to view things differently. Don't get stuck in a rut, doing life and merely going through the motions. Be open to a new tomorrow. Entertain a new way of thinking. Train your mind to see the good. It may not be how you're used to doing life, but today is a good day to do things differently. Remember, what you focus on flourishes.

Feed your creative focus. Starve your distractions, fears, and the drama. Don't get overwhelmed. Get focused. Don't look back. Focus forward. When life gets blurry, adjust your vision accordingly. Help others do the same. And know this: when you focus on the good, the good gets great.

YOUR PURSUIT

Focus on the positive and the possible to be *better than ever*.

CHAPTER 7

Seize the Day

"Don't wait for everything to be perfect before you decide to enjoy your life."

—JOYCE MEYER

The seven of us were in the living room—well, ten in total if you include the dogs, which, of course, I do. Two of my daughters were showing me the latest stunts they'd learned in gymnastics. My only son was harassing my oldest daughter to the point that she didn't think it was funny anymore. The dogs were running around the room barking and playing. On the television, the newscaster was about to announce the next president of the United States. The volume was blaring loud enough that I'm pretty sure my neighbors could hear it. Dogs barking, news blaring, and kids on the verge of fighting. My two young, budding gymnasts must have said, "Mom! Watch!" for the zillionth time. To say it was chaotic in my house that night would be a substantial understatement. I busied myself trying to settle the fight, quiet the dogs, watch cartwheels, and pay attention to the world event declarations on the way-too-loud television.

Smack dab in the middle of all the above-described chaos, my youngest daughter handed me a picture she'd drawn. "Just for you,

Mom," she said. She'd drawn me and her standing together. We both had long hair and big smiles on our faces. She'd also taken the time to capture us both wearing really cute shoes. (I taught her well!) The emotional clincher was written in crayon across the top of her little masterpiece: "MOMMY, I LOVE YOU."

Now I know, if you're a parent, you've probably received many of these awesome kid-created portraits. But you have to admit, the timing of her artwork presentation was...well...something else. Arriella didn't care what was happening on the news. She couldn't have cared less about who was to be the next president. She wasn't bothered about the dogs or her brother and sister fighting. She wasn't even interested in her sisters' latest stunts. The only thing Arriella cared about in that moment of unbelievable chaos was that I knew one incredibly important thing: *Mommy, I love you.*

From the mouths of babes. My youngest wanted me to know I was loved. No agenda, no expectation. Pure and simple. She loved me. My daughter's picture and her refusal to be distracted from the raging river of chaos around her was a wonderful reminder of what really matters. Life is about those we choose to share it with. It's about the love we have for each other. It's about all of these little moments. I still remain grateful for that little moment as it's one I won't ever forget.

Too often we get so caught up in our various activities that we forget to stop and enjoy today. We get wrapped up in *doing* and we lose sight of *being*. Maybe you can relate to this prayer that I often read:

Dear Lord,

So far today, I am doing all right. I have not gossiped, lost my temper, been greedy, grumpy, nasty, selfish, or self-indulgent. I have not whined, cursed, or eaten any chocolate. However, I am going to get out of bed in a few minutes, and I will need a lot more help after that.

Amen

We all know that life can get hectic. It's like a roller coaster ride full of ups and downs. Sometimes we even scream along the way. I don't know about you, but, as I've said before, I'm not sure if life is passing me by, or if it's trying to run me over! We get so busy thinking about the future and everything we have to get done, or fretting over the past, wishing we would've done things differently, that we oftentimes lose sight of the present. The Bible lets us know that "This *is* the day the Lord has made; we will rejoice and be glad in it." (Psalm 118:24 NKJV). Another translation of the same verse says, "I will celebrate and be happy in it." I love that statement! Not only does God have a plan for our lives, but He has a plan for every day of our lives.

Sure, He has a great future in store for each of us, but equally as exciting to me is that He also has a great *today* in store for us. He's concerned about the big things, but He is also concerned about the small things. God wants to be involved in our today. He has given us today to enjoy. It truly is a gift. How we choose to live in the present is totally up to us. It's key to how today goes, and how we can make every day that follows ***better than ever***.

What are you doing today to be intentional about enjoying your day? No matter what happens, there's no way to ensure that everything in your life will go great, that the sky will be eternally blue, that the kids will be perfectly behaved, and that gratitude will drive your household without a challenging moment. We're also not talking about dealing with your background, your current life situation, the size of your house, or even the amount of money you have in the bank.

We're talking about how you choose to look at today. *This day.*

I love what Jim Carrey says. "I think everybody should get rich and famous and do everything they ever dreamed of so they can see that it's not the answer." Oprah also nailed it when she said, "Having the best things is no substitute for having the best life." So, again I ask: How will you choose to live fully and enjoy this day? I want to encourage you. Don't get so busy making a living that you forget to make a life. Love those God has placed before you. He's put them there for a reason. Never take people for granted. God didn't give us family as a burden, but instead, to grow us and lift us up. He has given us grace for everything we're going to face in life. The thing we have to do is make sure we don't get so wrapped up in our to-do list that we lose sight of our "today is a gift, so enjoy it" list.

Today Is a Masterpiece

There's a miracle inside today. Be grateful for it! Some people didn't get a chance for another day, but we did. Take advantage of it. Don't waste your present. If you're experiencing a rough season, then you might be wondering exactly how today could be worthy of being labeled a miracle. Simply stated, you woke up. You're breathing. You have a pulse! Every second of every day that you're alive truly is a miracle. Don't overlook all the little miracles that are hiding in plain sight. This is about being present in the moment.

You can't have a better today if you keep thinking about yesterday. Yesterday is gone. Over. Done. You can't change it. You can't take it back. You can't make it go away. It's history. Now, that's not to say we aren't allowed to go back to a moment, reflect, learn, and grow. Just don't live there. Don't allow yesterday to take up so much of today that you lose it.

You may have lived through a bad yesterday, but the good news is that yesterday ended last night. This is a new day. The scriptures assure us that "The steadfast love of the Lord never ceases; His mercies never come to an end; they are new every morning; great is your faithfulness." (Lamentations 3:22–23 ESV) Now, that's pretty amazing.

Decide to own this day. It's a decision only you can make. How you live today is entirely within your power. You can choose how you act and react. The day will be what you make it. Jim Rohn said,

"Either you run the day, or the day runs you." Run your day! When you mess up, shake it off and keep going. When you face a challenge, don't get frustrated. Instead, trust that God is going to help you through. A bad moment doesn't mean the whole day has to be bad. Choose *happy*! Happiness is truly a choice. We all get the same twenty-four hours every single day. It's how we choose to live those hours that matter. Why not choose happy? Happiness isn't a destination. It's a way of life.

John Lennon once said, "When I was five years old, my mother always told me that happiness was the key to life. When I went to school, they asked me what I wanted to be when I grew up. I wrote down 'happy.' They told me I didn't understand the assignment, and I told them they didn't understand life." Today, you can find happy, be happy, and then *live* happy! It's not about your circumstances. Happiness is an inside job. Don't wait for someone else to bring happiness to you; find it from within. This day will be what you make of it. Make it a masterpiece. Love those around you. Be grateful for the gift of today. Enjoy your journey. Life doesn't have to get good for you to start enjoying it. You can chase happiness even today and when you do so, your life becomes ***better than ever***.

YOUR PURSUIT

Find joy in today and watch the days get *better than ever*.

CHAPTER 8

Find Your Eagles

"People inspire you, or they drain you—pick them wisely."

—HANS F. HANSEN

Let me ask you something. Who are your people? Who are the individuals you're closest to, the ones you allow to speak into your life? Who are the folks you go to when you need some encouragement, wisdom, or advice? I'm going to guess I'm not the only one who has heard this saying: "You become like the five people you hang around with most. So, choose wisely." Sounds good, right? Well, allow me to take that even a step further. I sincerely believe that you are only *as good* as the people you surround yourself with. That's why it's so important that you become intentional about who you let inhabit your environment.

We must be intentional about our inner circle, those chosen few that we allow inside our space. After all, we can show them who we really are, blemishes and all, and know beyond a shadow of a doubt that they'll still stick around. We only get one lifetime. It matters who we spend time with. We need to become picky about our people! We need to find individuals who bring out the best in us. Folks who make us smile. Those who make us laugh. People who inspire us to have big dreams. Human beings who stir up the God-given destiny that waits inside of us.

Our lives change for the better when we begin to hang out with next-level people. Not that long ago, I was speaking at an event. A well-known speaker (like *really* well known...like you'd know this person if I mentioned them) was in the audience. I was excited, but also anxious. It was a person I listened to regularly. An individual who inspires me and challenges me to do bigger and better things. I was suddenly standing in front of one of my mentors, who didn't really know I existed. I had no idea when I was invited to speak at this event that this person would end up not only being there, but that they would be sitting front and center, listening to me. I'd be lying if I said that didn't make me nervous because it certainly did. I think I might've even perspired a bit more than usual! Now, here's where it got interesting. Various thoughts started racing through my mind and then fear started creeping in. I had to really work to disengage with the swarm of negative notions that were desperate to take me captive.

As is probably the norm, the worst part was in the waiting. Backstage, as I prepared to go on, my comfort level went from bad to worse. Then as I was being introduced, I had to face my fear. Believe me, I thought about trying to get out of it, but only for a brief second. My fear was real, and it was really strong. I had to fight through the mind games as I made my way to the stage.

I'm thrilled to say, I did it! And believe it or not, I think it was one of my best speaking moments. Who would've thought? What helped me through? I believe it was that person sitting in the audience and a whole lot of fear! Haha! Sometimes we need to feel a bit of fear to raise our game to the next level. The anxiety that I was experiencing made me try a little harder. And wouldn't you know it? As I was speaking, I was actually aware of the fact that I was challenging myself to do better. I was telling myself to communicate at a good, strong pace and reminding myself not to move too fast. I was trying extra hard to speak as clearly as I could. (Some people think I have a Texas accent, but I just don't hear it!) The farther into my talk I got, surprisingly enough, the more confident I became. When I was finished, I felt like I had done a better job than I'd ever done in the past. After the event, my special audience member approached me and actually ended up speaking some really incredible things into my life, for which I will always be grateful.

I realized two amazing concepts that night. First, I actually had another level inside me. Second, I needed to be pushed by someone I respected and admired to get to my *A* game. I delivered a personal best that night. Consequently, I felt that I had delivered excellence to my audience. What an amazing feeling! That experience made me want to grow and continue to push myself, to constantly work to be ***better than ever***. In fact, that night, with all its wonderful memories, still drives me to work toward being an expert in the field God has graciously allowed me to inhabit and grow within.

The people in our lives should challenge the comfort *out* of us. They should cause us to be uncomfortable being comfortable. That's truly the only way authentic growth can happen. And if, for whatever reason, you aren't able to be with people like that, the internet is a great source for wisdom. There are some incredible people who have podcasts and books that can be truly beneficial. I have many mentors in my life via podcast. These people speak into my life every single day. It costs me nothing monetarily, but it does require discipline on my part to want to learn and grow. This type of input requires me to schedule time daily to allow them access and to allow them to speak into my life. Our people should be able to speak the good stuff, hard stuff, challenging stuff, and other stuff that will cause us to be better. Our community should challenge us to level up.

Listen to Those Who Challenge You to Be Better

When we surround ourselves with the right people, they can speak to things in our lives that we may not even see. Years ago, my sister Lisa and I were on a trip. As we were talking, she mentioned someone who stirred something up on the inside of me that I didn't know was still there. I quickly said something negative about that person. As I was speaking, my mind was questioning my words with, *Where in the world did this come from? Why are you saying this?* The next day, Lisa told me she wanted to talk to me.

She said, "April, what came out of your mouth about so-and-so was totally not like you. It was completely out of character for who you are. I just want to speak into your life and tell you that you need to get free of those feelings and have forgiveness in your heart toward that person and allow God to clean the slate. Because if you allow that to stay in your heart, the anointing of God will only be at a certain level in your life. And because of unforgiveness, you will never be at the place God has designed for you to walk in."

Yes, that's tough to hear. But immediately, I knew that she was speaking to me with truth and love. Because a hard, challenging, uncomfortable fact was spoken by one of my trusted people, I made things right in both myself and in that relationship. Once I did, I instantly felt the difference. The crazy part is that I didn't even know those feelings of unforgiveness were still inside of me. They were hiding on my blind side. I thank God that I had the right person around who wasn't afraid to speak a word of correction and insight. I was able to be called out, challenged, and then deal with it. The happy result was that I was completely set free from something that should have never been on the inside of me in the first place.

When you hang around people who challenge you to rise higher, grow, not stay in the same place, push you, and encourage you, you'll become a different person. We benefit in a multitude of ways when we surround ourselves with our own specific tribe. You've probably heard the saying, "If you hang out with chickens, you're gonna cluck. If you hang out with eagles, you're gonna soar." Find your eagles. Find the next-level people around you who are wiser, smarter, and more knowledgeable. Because who you surround yourself with really does say a lot about you.

Consider this. If you hang out with nine losers, what are your chances of becoming the tenth? Ouch! Recognize that some people who've been a part of your history might not belong in your destiny. If they aren't adding to your life, perhaps you should consider letting go of those who are weighing you down. Step away from the dream stealers, naysayers, and happiness takers. The scripture states: "If you want to grow in wisdom, spend time with the wise. Walk with the wicked and you'll eventually become just like them." (Proverbs 13:20 TPT) Wow! In other words, show me your friends and I'll show you your future.

You can't change others, but you can change who you choose to be around. Change will always begin with you. Be picky about your people. Today is a good day to evaluate who inhabits your life. It's an even better day to make a change. Your people circle might get smaller, but who knows? Your vision just might get bigger.

YOUR PURSUIT

Surround yourself with people who bring out your best to make your life *better than ever*.

CHAPTER 9

Break the Cycle

"You are one decision away from a totally different life."

—MARK BATTERSON

My father was born in 1921, in Paris…Paris, Texas, that is. He was the youngest of six kids and was raised on a cotton farm. His family didn't have much to start with, but when the Great Depression hit, the little they had dropped to almost nothing. My dad and his siblings would go days without much to eat and many times he was sent to school with only a small biscuit to nibble on for the whole day. He often had to stand in long lines waiting for free milk and food. Times were tough.

When my dad got older and had a family of his own, he was determined that his children would never face the poverty that he'd experienced as a child. He knew his parents had tried and done the best that they could. He was grateful for them and all their efforts to provide for him and his siblings, but he sure didn't want his family to know what "barely making it" felt like. He decided to do whatever was necessary to break the cycle of poverty in our family line once and for all. He was determined not to repeat the mistakes of the past. He wanted to demonstrate that the past had no power over him anymore. That determination allowed my family to grow up in a blessed and prosperous home, one that I am grateful for and desire to pass down to my children.

I love that Daddy knew change began with him. He realized he could either keep living a life of poverty or take a stand against it. He decided that poverty continued to run in the family, until it ran into him. This one decision to be the one to break the cycle changed the course of his life and the lives of his family for future generations.

It's our choice how we choose to spend the rest of our lives. We can spend it repeating cycles, doing the same things we've always done, wishing things were different, but not doing anything to bring about positive results. Or we can take charge and change things. If we keep doing the same thing, we will keep getting the same result. We can't wish ourselves out of any situation. We have to make the decisions that declare unhealthy patterns stop with us. We have to stand up and say that negative behavior and unhealthy behavior are no longer welcome in our families. It's going to take some backbone, but we can do it.

Once we make that decision, it doesn't matter what traits, habits, or hindrances have been passed down to us. We can break the cycle. We can make the choice not to repeat past behaviors that aren't conducive to living joyous, happy lives. We have to stand firm that we aren't going to repeat the past if the past isn't worth repeating.

After all, the past is a place of reference, not a place of residence.

The Importance of Showing Love and Appreciation

An elderly man was lying in a hospital bed. Although he was medicated, he was coherent and aware when someone entered his room. He couldn't see who the person was, but he assumed it was the doctor. Nearing the end of his life, he was flooded with emotional thoughts concerning his family.

He spoke out in a soft but determined voice, "Doctor, have I told you about my son?"

The doctor eagerly came to the elderly man's bedside. The old man took his hand and politely asked him to sit down. "Oh doctor, let me tell you about my boy. I'm so proud of him. He's grown up to be a remarkable man. You know he was a great football player—one of the best on the team. He never gave his mother or me any trouble, and he was such a joy to raise. I can honestly tell you he is the best son a father could possibly have."

After a little while, the man began to get tired. He patted the doctor's hand and said, "I just wanted to let you know about my son and how much I love him."

He slowly let go of his hand and thanked the doctor for listening. Without saying a word, the doctor quietly walked toward the door, never taking his eyes off of the elderly man. He wanted to remember the moment. After all, he'd waited a lifetime to hear it. The reality was, this doctor wasn't really a doctor at all. He was actually the man's son—the very one he was talking about. During all the years of growing up, his father had never expressed his love for his son, let alone that he was proud of him. Oh sure, the son knew, deep down, that his dad loved him, but he just wanted to hear him say it. Finally, as his dad was slipping away, he heard the words he had so desperately longed to hear. And even as a grown man, those words brought life and strength to his heart.

Whenever I think about this story, it reminds me of the importance of showing love and telling our family we love them and not waiting for life to get near the end before we do so. Our words can bring healing, but they only do so if they're spoken. Maybe you didn't receive affection from your parents while growing up. Perhaps you, in turn, are repeating the pattern of not showing affection and not expressing your love to your children. It's time to initiate a shift in your patterns. Guess what? You're no longer a victim of what you've been through. You're one decision away from a totally different life.

If you want a different result, make a different choice. Your family needs to know you're their biggest cheerleader. They need to know you're for them. They yearn to hear you say you're proud of them and you believe in them.

I challenge you to be brave enough to step out of your comfort zone and be better than what broke you. Be better than what is holding you back. Be better than the patterns that have been passed down to you. Set a better pattern for your family. Shift from being awkward about affection and give someone you love a hug. Shift away from being silent and actually say, "I love you."

It all starts with making the decision.

Sure, it might be uncomfortable at first, but at least you're taking a step in the right direction. Find the necessary mentors who can help you, people who can provide a Godly example for you. If you desire to be a better parent, hang around parents that you admire. Observe their lifestyles. Find out what makes their homes special. Ask them questions. Be a student of what you admire. I once heard a pastor say when he first had kids, he didn't know how to be a good father because he came from a very abusive background. His father didn't show love at all, and in fact, he couldn't even remember his father ever telling him that he loved him. This pastor never heard the words, "I love you." When he found himself with kids of his own, he just didn't know what to do. He felt totally unprepared. He felt like a failure. All that changed when he realized that his best friend also happened to be an excellent father. This man loved his kids, spent time with them, smothered them in love and affection. He also loved his wife and treated her the same way. It dawned on the pastor that the best way to learn a new, Godly pattern could be as simple as emulating his friend. And for the next few months, that's exactly what he did. He became the student, watching and learning. It wasn't too long before he felt comfortable being a father who could show love to his kids and who was no longer hesitant to show them affection in public or private. He told them every single day, multiple times, how much he loved them. Slowly, by first becoming a student, he was able to break the pattern that had broken him as a young boy. I'm happy to say that this pastor never turned back. I'm sure the lives of his kids were transformed because of it.

Stop the Cycle for the Children

If you don't like your story, change it. Choose compassion. Choose unconditional love. Choose empathy. Choose forgiveness. Choose mercy and grace. Be the person you needed when you were going through the stuff of life. Set a new course. Form a new habit. Create a better legacy for your children. Remember, they're watching and learning from your behavior. Healthy patterns teach them to thrive in life. Unhealthy patterns show them how to survive. When you don't face issues that have been passed down, you allow those issues to move down in the generations to your children. Broken parents set the foundation for broken children. What you choose to do really does matter because every decision has the power to set you up to be ***better than ever***.

On December 1, 1955, Rosa Parks did something that shocked the world. When a white bus driver told her and three other African-American riders to move from the middle of the bus to the back, Rosa decided not to obey, even though the three others complied. In her memoir, *Rosa Parks: My Story*, Mrs. Parks said she sensed an unusual resolve well up inside her at that moment. She wrote:

> *"When that white driver stepped back toward us, when he waved his hand and ordered us up and out of our seats, I felt a determination cover my body like a quilt on a winter night."*

When Rosa refused, the bus driver said, "I'm going to have you arrested."

"You may do that," Rosa responded in a respectful but matter-of-fact tone.

The passage of civil rights laws swept the nation because of one woman's willingness to sit down in order to stand up for what was right. She would settle for nothing less than being all that God had created her to be.

"People always say that I didn't give up my seat because I was tired, but that isn't true. I was not tired physically, or no more tired than I usually was..." Mrs. Parks said. "The only tired I was, was tired of giving in."

This woman's story will never lose its power to inspire me. The courage of this amazing woman to stand up for what she knew wasn't right is one of the most powerful moments in American history. She decided to take a stand regardless of the cost, knowing full well that there most certainly would be a cost that could include being beaten or even killed for her actions. When Mrs. Parks stood up for the right thing, the Godly thing, she ended up changing the course of history. She broke the cycle. This history-maker and world-changer blazed a trail for future generations and for true freedom for all people.

There are so many things I love about her, but the one thing that stands out above the rest is that Rosa Parks had a made-up mind. She was decisive. She was a change-maker. She was done with the old and ready for something new to take place. She had taken stock and weighed the cost and still decided that she would stand for right. What an incredible lady.

Mrs. Parks said: "I have learned over the years that when one's mind is made up, this diminishes fear." If that doesn't speak to the power of a made-up mind and the decision to break the cycle, I don't know what will. So let me ask you something. What are you wanting to see differently in your life? How would you like to see your present situation or current circumstances change? What are you believing God for? Whatever it might be, get it in your heart. Get a made-up mind that nothing and no one will keep you from what you desire to see.

In other words, know what you believe and don't stray from it. Don't allow anyone else, including yourself, to convince you otherwise. Your mind can be your greatest ally or your biggest detractor. Your success or ultimate failure can rest in the power of your made-up mind. You see, your mind will either be for you or against you. It will be your greatest asset or your greatest enemy. There's nothing in this world that can trouble you as much as your own thoughts. That's why you have to know what you want, know what you believe, and you have to stick to it. Commit. A made-up mind seldom turns.

Break the Cycle of Fear

Don't be afraid to take steps out of the ordinary to make your life ***better than ever***. Look at Rosa Parks. She sat down to stand up for what was right. It's okay to be different. It's okay to do what you feel in your heart is the right thing to do. It's your life and your dreams. It's okay to make the decision to change.

Let me make it even more practical. If you have a made-up mind to lose weight, don't surround yourself with food that isn't going to help you on your journey. Picture yourself at a healthy weight and then set yourself up to succeed. Get a made-up mind and break the cycle.

If you have a made-up mind to get out of debt, then stop spending money and begin to live beneath your means. Ouch! That hurts, I know, because those shoes are so cute! Instead, get a vision of being completely out of debt. Get a plan and then work your plan. Have a made-up mind that nothing is going to cause you to stray. You can break the cycle.

If you're trying to get beyond a broken heart, don't listen to every sad break-up song that was ever made in the history of time! There's somebody out there who's going to love you for the incredible person *you* are! Put some happy music on. Get back into life and act like the amazing person God designed you to be. Just because someone didn't see your worth doesn't mean you aren't valuable. You can break the cycle.

You can take steps to change your situation and make your life ***better than ever*** when you:

Don't talk defeat.
Don't talk doubt.
Don't talk yourself down.
Don't let anyone talk you out of it.
Don't let circumstances discourage you from thinking that you can achieve your goals.

Most importantly, *don't be afraid*. Fear doesn't stop death. It stops life, living, and achieving the things that you desire. Don't adapt to your environment, change it. Don't think of all the reasons it won't happen, think of how you will act and react when it does. Set your mind and keep it set. Don't stop until you see your desires come to pass. Be consistent. Consistency doesn't mean you won't mess up, it just means that you'll never *give* up. Hey, it may not be easy, but it'll be well worth it.

Get your words working for you and not against you. Stop saying, "I'll never." Start saying, "I will." Stop saying, "I can't." Instead, say, "I can." Stop saying, "It won't happen." Repeat, as often as necessary: "It will happen." Small tweaks lead to big peaks!

You can do it.
You are strong.
You are capable.
You can do more than you know.

Never overestimate what's going on around you or underestimate what is inside of you. Decide what you want and where you want to be. Stick to it. Do something today that will make your future self proud. Don't be afraid to go after the life you want to live.

Remember, the life in front of you is way more important than what has happened behind you.

When you strive for change, you're not only breaking the cycle for yourself, but for generations to come. Just like my dad did. The decision doesn't mean everything will instantly be perfect. But nothing can change without the decision. That's the first step. Decide that you're not going to allow your past to dictate your future. Your new mantra can be, "It ran in the family, until it ran into me!" Break the cycle. Become the best version of yourself you can be. Become the best father, mother, son, or daughter you've ever seen. Become the best student, employee, or boss you've ever heard of.

You have the power to bring about change. Be courageous and step out of the cycle that has been passed down to you. Confront, deal, and change it. Take a stand and say, "No, I'm choosing a different path for me and my family."

Rewrite the narrative of your story. Realize that just because you didn't come from a healthy family doesn't mean a healthy family can't come from you. Life really is what you make it. Don't live with regret. Tell your family how much you love them every single day. Give them a hug! Today is the day to plant a new family tree. Life is too short. Seize every moment. You can become the change you need for a better life. You may not be able to change the past, but you're one decision away from changing your future. Always remember: You're leaving a legacy. Make sure it's one you can be proud of.

YOUR PURSUIT

Change what you don't like or want to become *better than ever*.

CHAPTER 10

It's the Thought that Counts

"Your thoughts are the architects of your destiny."

—DAVID O. MCKAY

When I was a pastor, I decided to hold a meeting for all of the ladies in our church. It was going to be the first time anything like it had been done at my church. I wanted the gathering to be amazing. I assembled a wonderful, creative team around me. We planned ferociously and began working toward a night the ladies would never forget. I was beyond excited. I felt well prepared and was really dialed in on my chosen topic. The team members all had their tasks well underway. Everything was on point and we still had a few days until the event was to take place.

Unfortunately, it was then that I inadvertently did something that turned things in the wrong direction. I started thinking! I know, it sounds silly, but that's precisely what happened. I chose to overthink and caused myself all manner of grief. I can promise you it was solely my thoughts that were causing me to sink into a strange abyss. And I mean fast.

Of course, I started worrying. I began to wonder if anyone would even show up to our Chik Nite (as we called it). The more I thought, the more I worried, and the more I worried, the worse it got. *What if things go wrong? What if they don't want to hear what I have to say? What if no one wants to come to hear my topic at all?* My mind was filled with nightmarish visions of the entire assembly ending in complete and total disaster. Oh, trust me. It was bad. One thought led to another, worse than the one before, and I began to actually believe that I probably should have never, ever planned the night in the first place. I can't begin to tell you what staggering discouragement I felt. It was all I could think about.

Little by little, I was thinking myself *out* of the very event that I'd created. I was thinking myself down to less than nothing. I became more and more discouraged with each passing negative thought. I was actually disqualifying myself, before I even stepped onto the playing field. I'd almost convinced myself that I shouldn't go on with the event, which was fast evolving into thoughts that I *couldn't* go through with it.

One morning, in the midst of my personal meltdown, I was home with my youngest, Arriella. She was about four years old at the time. We were in my bathroom and I was sitting at my vanity, contemplating putting on some makeup. The truth was, I was so heavy-hearted and burdened down with worry and concern, I didn't much feel like doing anything. My daughter was playing behind me on the floor when suddenly she stood up, and out of nowhere, said very clearly and loudly, "Mommy, the devil is just a chicken."

My first thought was, *What in the world! Where did that even come from?* Then I looked right at her and said, "What did you just say?"

She put her hand on her hip and, with a little bit of sassy attitude, pointed her finger right at me and said again, "The devil is just a chicken!"

I felt like I had just been corrected by my four-year-old! Her little voice hit me like a ton of bricks. And even though her statement to me was random and out of the blue, at that moment, I realized that God was providing me with a valuable life lesson. And, of all things, He was using my four-year-old to do it! Isn't that just like God? That one little phrase cut me deep. I interpreted her statement this way: *April, the God on the inside of you is greater than the fear that's surrounding you. The devil is trying to discourage you from all that God has planned for you. You got this. God is with you, for you, and in you. You have to remember, the devil ain't all that. He's just a chicken!*

That's all I needed. I found my (momentarily misplaced) spiritual backbone and began to remind myself of who I am in Christ. I stopped thinking those discouraging, negative, self-defeating thoughts. I turned my thought life around so it could start working for me, instead of against me. Every time fear came into my mind, I reminded myself that God was for me. It was time for *me* to stop being against me.

We had our Chik Nite. I'm happy to say nearly a thousand beautiful women showed up and experienced an evening filled with love, laughter, and fun. Women's lives were changed that night, not because of any single person, but because a band of women stood together praying for one another and speaking life into each other. It was truly a night to remember.

I'm so grateful God used my little girl to get me back on track. My thoughts almost prevented that meeting from happening. My feelings almost got in the way of something new God wanted to do. Fear almost won, but thanks to God, it didn't.

Your Mind Believes You

I share this story to explain just how important your thoughts are. What you think about yourself matters. Scripture tells us, "As [a man] thinks in his heart, so is he." (Proverbs 23:7 AMP) In other words, what you think will eventually burrow down into your heart. Furthermore, what's in your heart will always come out of your mouth. That's why the way you talk to and about yourself matters *a lot*. You have to be careful about how you talk to yourself, because *you* are listening. Understand that you'll never speak to anyone more than you silently (or maybe even subconsciously) speak to yourself.

The average person has forty thousand thoughts a day. Amazingly, 80 percent of those thoughts are negative! No wonder our world is in the state it is in. Thoughts are not facts. Often, they create problems that weren't there in the first place. Mark Twain said it well: "I've suffered a great many catastrophes in my life. Most of them never happened." Your mind believes everything you feed it. If you feed it negativity, you'll live a negative life. If you feed it worry, you'll be burdened and stressed out. It's important that we continually feed our minds life, faith, vision, encouragement, hope, love, grace, and mercy.

The enemy will hardly miss an opportunity to discourage you. He'll plant a thought in your mind to try to convince you that you're not capable, you're not talented, you'll never be successful, or that your family will never be happy again. He's a liar. We *have* to take every thought captive. In other words, don't believe everything you think! Our thoughts really do matter. We have to think about what we're thinking about. We have to be proactive in thinking good thoughts.

Muhammad Ali believed that. He said, "I am the greatest. I said that even before I knew I was. I figured that if I said it enough, I would convince the world that I really was the greatest." As he proves, you can become what you believe about yourself. It's time to start thinking differently about yourself. Start believing in yourself to make your life ***better than ever***.

In order to cultivate better thinking, more than likely, you're going to have to do some renovations. Here are some things to think about:

- Stop being your own worst critic. There are enough critics in this world.

- Stop thinking the negative thoughts. When a negative thought comes, recognize and reject it.
- Shake off the negativity that's been spoken over you. No more listening to it!
- Stop allowing other people to decide who you are. You're not who they say you are.
- You're who God says you are.

When an unhealthy or negative beat of self-talk creeps into your brain, decide to stop it dead in its tracks. You have the power. Use it. Change your thoughts and you'll change your life for the better. The great thing is, just like that, you can make a change. Just like that, you can change the course of your life and your day. You don't need a new day to start over. You can start right now. Always remember who you are, and then, every single day, start showing up as that person. And just in case you forget, let me remind you: the devil is just a chicken!

YOUR PURSUIT

Give yourself thoughts of love, grace, and mercy to make your days *better than ever*.

CHAPTER 11

Lighten Up

"Don't take life too seriously. You'll never get out of it alive."

—ELBERT HUBBARD

A few years back, my perspective on life (and what's really important) shifted. Why and how that happened is something I'll never forget. It was a Sunday morning, and we were all getting ready for church, just like we had for an entire lifetime of Sundays. Things were going well, for the most part, until one of my kids decided to flush the toilet.

All of a sudden, my middle daughter, Savannah, screamed, "Mom!"

It startled me, of course, and I ran into the bathroom only to discover that the toilet had overflowed. Water was pouring out of the bowl. By the time I reached the doorway, the entire bathroom floor was nearly submerged. It was awful. Of course, on this occasion, I happened to be already fully dressed and suddenly found myself standing in my really cute, now also fully submerged, shoes. (A moment of silence for the shoes is needed.) You can imagine my frustration. I was calling out for help while the kids were running around, ignoring my pleas. It was like a circus. Bad, right? Well, you haven't heard the half of it yet.

Just a few minutes later, high-pitched screams rang out from the upstairs. "*Mom*!" was echoing throughout the entire house. I ran upstairs and, believe it or not, another toilet was overflowing! It was crazy. The house was in an uproar. We were all running around, throwing towels on the floor. The kids were slipping and falling in the water and I was getting soaked.

Just as we started to get things under control, my son, Garrison, yelled from downstairs, "Mom, come quick. *Hurry*!"

We all headed to the downstairs bathroom. Just as we opened the door, the vent in the ceiling gave up the ghost and collapsed under the pressure from the water above. Our downstairs bathroom was instantly transformed into a wonderful, cascading waterfall! It was official. The toilet demon had entered our house and we had no idea if he was finished or not. Standing there, almost in disbelief of everything that'd just taken place, I began to look around. I quickly assessed the mess, calculated the many loads of laundry I would be doing after church, and cringed at the thought of all of us having to change clothes. The reality was, I wanted to cry. But then it happened. Suddenly, amid all the mess, I began to laugh. And I don't mean just a light-hearted giggle. It was coming from the deep pit of my soul. It was one of those belly laughs that make your stomach hurt after the fact. I can't even explain it. I definitely surprised myself!

I think the situation had gotten so bad that it actually became staggeringly funny to me. Hesitantly, my kids cracked slight smiles, almost as if they weren't exactly sure if it was safe or not to laugh with me. Finally, when they realized it was okay, we all burst out laughing again while gazing at the destruction and monumental mess before us.

I'll never forget that day. In fact, I don't think any of us will. I wish I could say I always react that way: laughing instead of crying or yelling, or both. It was only by the grace of God that it happened that way on that particular day. I guess the reality is that times get tough, things get ugly (and smelly), and often the unexpected happens. It's easy to just go with our natural reaction. But...what if there's another way?

Gaining Life with Laughter

What if, in the midst of a difficult time, we made an effort to do something other than what's expected? What if, in the midst of all of the mess, we changed our perspective? I mean, were toilets overflowing really the end of the world for me? It may have seemed so at the moment, but in the big scheme of things, it essentially wasn't. I still had my house and health. We still made it to church that day (a little late, but still). We made it through.

Let me ask you something. When was the last time you laughed? And I'm not talking about using one of those silly smiley-face emojis or even sharing a brief little half-laugh. I mean, like *really* laughed, like a my-stomach-hurts-from-laughing-so-hard event?

Let's be honest. Sometimes, life gets so busy. We become so consumed with everything that we still have to do (probably more often than we'd like to admit) that we forget to stop, breathe deeply, smile, or even laugh at something crazy that life has thrown us. And before we know it, we live lives as "human *do*ings" and not as "human *be*ings."

I believe God has much more in store for us. He doesn't just want us to live day to day, without any joy or laughter. He wants every single day to be ***better than ever***. John 10:10 says He wants us to live life to the full, in abundance, until it overflows. Life without laughter certainly doesn't sound either abundant or overflowing to me. Perhaps, it's time to lighten up and start laughing again!

In the Bible, Sarah laughed when God told her she was going to have a baby at ninety years of age. I'd be laughing too! I bet she laughed again when that beautiful baby was born, but that time with pure joy. Do you know laughing one hundred times has the same effect on the body as being on a stationary bike for fifteen minutes? Not only that, but a daily dose of laughter can burn up to five pounds of fat over the course of a year. Hey, if we'd just laugh, instead of worrying, we'd all be skinnier! There's so much to gain from laughter.

Here are some of the things laughter can do:

- It boosts your mood. I mean, come on, you know you can't feel anxious, angry, or sad when you're laughing.
- It helps you get through tough times.
- It helps you to release stress and allows you the ability to stay focused so you can accomplish more.
- It reduces blood pressure and improves blood flow.
- It fuels your immune system.
- It draws you closer to others.
- It's good for your emotional and mental health.
- It essentially recharges your battery.

Laughter just might be exactly what you need to relax and stop being so uptight! One minute of anger weakens your immune system for four to five hours, while one minute of laughter boosts it for twenty-four. Now that's a good reason to laugh more and frown less. On top of all of these statistics, laughter makes you feel better overall! Maybe it's time to stop getting your panties in a ruffle or your boxers in a bunch! (You know which one you are.)

Now, we all know laughter doesn't always come easy. Sometimes we'll have to be intentional about it. Yep, I'm saying sometimes we have to laugh on purpose and allow ourselves to laugh regularly.

You'll be amazed at how this one act forces you to be fully present in the moment. Laughter really does allow us to enjoy life a little more. It helps us to take life less seriously. It encourages us to let down our guard, if even for a few minutes. Having trouble getting started? Try smiling! Smiling is the proverbial set of training wheels to laughter. Another valuable concept concerning laughter is that it is, quite frequently, contagious.

Want practical ways to practice? Find fun people who like to laugh, and spend time with them. Evaluate your circle. Are they all serious? Does anybody laugh? If the answer is no, then get out there with humorous folks who enjoy life and love to laugh.

Finding Funny Material

I realize that some of you might be thinking you have nothing to laugh about. If so, I'll have to share one of my secrets with you. Ready? *Laugh at yourself.* If you're at all like me, you've probably got some really good material. Just the other day, I sent a friend a text, thanking her for some things she'd done for me. I put my heart into that text and was happy to send it off to her first thing in the morning. I thought it'd start her day on a positive note. Later that day, I reread the text, only to discover that instead of putting, "you're the best," autocorrect changed it to "you're the *beast.*" *Lord help us all.* But you know what? We had a really good laugh over that text. It's something we'll laugh about for a good while, I'm sure.

I was in a Starbucks drive-through line in Dallas and had just given the guy my order. The employee repeated the order, thanked me, and told me he'd see me at the window. I was rolling up my window and before I knew it, I said, "Ok, thank you... *love you.*" (I don't know what it is about drive-throughs, but Lord have mercy!) *Did I just tell the Starbucks guy that* I loved him*?* I was mortified. I tried to get out of that line, but I was stuck with cars in front and behind me. Finally, it was my turn. I rolled down my window and could barely turn my head to look at the guy. There he was, young and good looking. I suddenly wished my girls were in the car with me. He had a smile as big as Texas, pearly white teeth, and the first thing out of his mouth was, "So you love me, do you?" I can't even begin to tell you how embarrassed I was. I wanted to say, "Just be quiet and give me my coffee!" Instead, I smiled with a red face, got my coffee, told him I loved everyone in the whole wide world. I sped off and have never, ever, ever been back to that Starbucks again.

Let me assure you, when you can laugh at yourself, there's absolute freedom. There's a saying that goes, "Blessed are those who can laugh at themselves, for they will not cease to be amused." Allow me to encourage you. Don't go a day without laughing. The scripture tells us that, "A merry heart does good, like medicine, but a broken spirit dries the bones." (Proverbs 17:22 NKJV) It's hard to be depressed when you're laughing. Bring laughter into your home. Fire up a funny movie or television show. Do something with your family that brings joy and laughter. Some of my fondest memories growing up are the times my family and I were together and laughing. Honestly, when we all get together even now, it seems like we spend most of our time laughing. Laughter is good for the soul. It will always be the best form of therapy. Once you start laughing, you just might start healing. Life is too short to be serious all of the time and it's always better when you're laughing.

And hey, just in case no one has told you today, You're the *beast*!

YOUR PURSUIT

Find people, situations, and reasons to laugh, and you'll make each day *better than ever*.

CHAPTER 12

Keep Walking

"You don't have to see the whole staircase, just take the first step."

—MARTIN LUTHER KING JR.

When I was about seven years old, we were on a family vacation on the beautiful big island of Hawaii. While my mom and dad were in meetings all week, my siblings and I took up residence at the nearest beach. To say it was gorgeous, with the white sand contrasting so starkly to the bright blue ocean, would be a massive understatement. It was our first time ever in Hawaii, and the trip was nothing short of amazing. We were all loving every minute of it.

After riding the waves on our little rented rafts for the larger part of that first morning, I decided it was time for a break. I laid back on my raft, thinking I'd enjoy some floating and resting. I know, the life of a seven-year-old is pretty rough (haha!), but an interesting thing happened when I opened my eyes after what felt like only a few seconds. I was instantly confused as I looked around and saw an empty beach. It looked like I was on a deserted island. Not one human being was to be seen. I mean *nobody*.

Surprisingly enough, I didn't panic. I simply stood up, put my little raft under my arm, and turned to the right, back toward where I figured I had come from. I started walking. I trudged along for what seemed like forever until finally, I saw signs of life. Way ahead in the distance, there were people on the beach playing ball. The ocean was filled with surfers and swimmers again. I can't begin to tell you how happy I was! That was about to change. In the distance, I saw my brothers and sisters packing up their towels as if they were going in for the day. When my brother Joel saw me, he pointed in my direction and the entire group came running toward me. I remember thinking how great and odd it was that they were so excited to see me. I mean, I was just with them. *Or so I thought.*

My oldest brother, Paul, was mad. "You go tell Mama and Daddy what you have done right now!"

I looked closely at everyone. They all seemed equal parts stressed and relieved. The joy of seeing me now seemed to be outweighed by the irritation they were feeling. We all began walking back toward the hotel so that I could tell my parents whatever it was that I'd done. The truth was, I had no clue what had transpired to get everyone so worked up to the point where my brother would actually yell at me. Little did I know, I'd fallen asleep on my raft and disappeared for hours! My siblings had looked frantically for me up and down the beach. They finally came to the grim conclusion that I must've drowned. By the time I came walking up, they were on their way to tell our parents that I was gone forever. After hearing their side of the story, it all made much more sense. I understood their irritation and my brother's anger. I couldn't even begin to imagine the unbelievable stress I'd put them through.

Now, as an adult, thinking about it sends chills down my spine. The thought of that same scenario happening to one of my kids, or one of my brothers or sisters, is too much to fathom. I completely understand why Paul was mad. I had been under his watch. He had carried the responsibility of losing his *favorite* little sister. What a way to spend our first day in beautiful Hawaii.

All I know for sure is God truly protected me on that day. Let's think about it. I could have floated way out to sea or even drowned. I know some serious angels were watching over me, keeping me close to the shore and helping me make it back safe and sound to my family. I'm so very grateful that I orchestrated the simple task of walking. Hey, I didn't know where I was going, but thank God my little seven-year-old self had the wherewithal to simply take a step, in any direction! Although I didn't know it in the moment, that tiny decision led me to safety and back into the arms of my family.

Put Feet to Your Faith

You might remember the story in the Bible (John 5:1–8) where Jesus went to the pool of Bethesda, a place where those who needed healing (the lame, blind, and paralyzed) gathered, waiting for an angel of the Lord to come and stir the waters. Whoever entered the waters first, while the waters were being stirred, would be healed. Jesus encountered a man who was paralyzed and had been lying by the waters for thirty-eight years. "Do you want to get well?" Jesus asked the man. He responded, "I have no one to help me into the pool when the water is stirred. While I am trying to get in, someone else goes down ahead of me."

This story has always intrigued me. I can understand five years of not being able to be the first one in the pool. I can even understand ten years, but thirty-eight years? After all that time, an angel comes by and you still aren't the first one in? Really? It seems like after ten years or so, you'd be laying so close to the edge of the water that all you had to do was slide your hand over into the pool. Or maybe you could even keep your big toe in there, just in case the angel might make a surprise appearance. But thirty-eight years of never being in the right place, at the right time? I'm sincerely glad that Jesus has more understanding and compassion than me.

He simply told the man, "Get up! Pick up your mat and walk."

And that's exactly what the man did. With the words spoken by Jesus, the guy picked up his mat and walked away from the place where he had been confined his whole life. Literally, he walked into a brand new life. What's interesting is that this man had to take action before he saw his miracle come to pass. He had to put feet to his faith.

Think about it. A paralyzed man had to get up and walk! Had he not acted in faith, he probably would've stayed in the same place, doing the same thing—lying by the pool—for thirty-eight additional years or more. Faith requires action. You have to get out of your comfort zone and do things you haven't done before. Sometimes we have to look for a way out, especially where there seem to be closed doors, locked windows, or brick walls. Believe me, I know often that's easier said than done. I know life happens.

Your spouse walks out on you. Your kids aren't doing well. You're in a job that you despise. You don't know how you're going to make it financially. The list goes on and on. It's really easy to get discouraged. Maybe you feel like that man by the pool, stuck in life, paralyzed by what you've gone through. Or maybe you just don't know what direction to go. Maybe you've said the same thing as this guy: "Nobody will help me."

Whatever your situation might be right now, know that where you are isn't permanent. You aren't stuck. You may feel like you are, but I'm telling you—and more importantly, the scripture is telling you—that you aren't. You may feel buried in life, bogged down by circumstances, maybe even filled with fear. That fear may be causing you to stay in the same place, tolerating the same conditions. I'm here to tell you that it's time to start walking. Even when you don't understand everything, even when you're filled with fear, even when you don't know which way to turn, get up, pick up your "raft," and start walking. What you're facing right now is no surprise to God. Even when you can't figure it all out, rest assured, He has it all sorted. The scripture says, "Since the Lord is directing our steps, why try to understand everything that happens along the way?" (Proverbs 20:24 TLB) Just get started. God has a solution for every problem. He's not stressed about it. He's not trying to punish you for where you've ended up. He's a good God and He cares about every detail of your life.

Part of trusting God is letting go of the unknown, including the unanswered questions, and saying, "God, I trust you. I believe You're working things out for my good. I believe all the pieces of the puzzle will one day make sense. I choose to trust and keep on walking through all of this."

In the Bible, God says, "I will never [under any circumstances] desert you [nor give you up nor leave you without support, nor will I in any degree leave you helpless], nor will I forsake or…relax my hold on you." (Hebrews 13:5 AMP, brackets from original source) You might just have to put this verse up on your bathroom mirror!

Others may have given up on you, deserted you, and even disappointed you. God isn't like that. He wants the best for you. He believes in you. He knows that when you get Him involved in your life, you can make it through anything. Do you want to get beyond your current situation in life? Then, it's time to put one foot in front of the other and start walking. Don't look back in fear. You're not going that way. Tune out those negative thoughts that keep you from moving forward and you'll take steps to make your life ***better than ever***. Stop listening to those bringing you down by telling you how you'll never make it through all of this. Let go of the excuses holding you back. Quit talking and start walking! *You* are stronger than you know. Winston Churchill said, "If you're going through hell, keep going." Yes, that means even though you're facing difficulties, keep going. Life isn't where you want it to be just yet? Keep walking. Bad things are happening? Keep moving. Even when you don't know how or when, take that first step and keep walking! Don't worry. God is preparing the way. You have what it takes. Grab a pair of good-looking shoes, strap them on, and walk this thing out. Sometimes you have to walk through the "blah" season to get to the "aha" season. Keep strutting, my friend. Your "aha" season is coming.

YOUR PURSUIT

Put feet to your faith to make your days *better than ever*.

CHAPTER 13

Do It Over

"If you don't like something, change it. If you can't change it, change your attitude. Don't complain."

—MAYA ANGELOU

I was coming home from a speaking engagement. My flight was running late. I realize that probably doesn't sound unusual for airline travel. It has certainly happened to me before, and it'll probably happen again. But this time, I can't even begin to tell you how meticulously I had planned out my schedule so this very thing wouldn't happen. I had thought and re-thought through every detail of my arrangements. I knew I had to finish up my speaking engagement in a timely manner, make it to the airport on time, fly home, pick up my youngest kids, and hurry straight to my daughter's championship volleyball game. It was state finals. She would be the one serving at the start of the game. There was no way I was going to miss it!

Just when I began to relax and believe everything was going to go according to schedule, the announcement came over the intercoms. That's right. My flight was delayed! Today of all days. In the entire history of my world, on any other day where this could have happened, the consequences would have been minimal. But this was not the day! I couldn't believe it was actually happening. I tried feverishly to find another flight, but there was nothing else available. I began to wonder if I would make it to the game *at all*. Talk about feeling like a bad mom.

Finally, we took off. As soon as we landed, I hurried off the plane and out of the terminal. I rushed to my car, raced home and scooped up my youngest kids, and quickly began the forty-five-minute drive to the game (*yes*, I said forty-five minutes!). As you might imagine, I was completely stressed out. I was bothered and worried. I was frustrated and annoyed. I just wanted to see my kid play in one of the most important games of her young life, and right at that moment, it didn't feel like I was going to get to see any part of the game at all. I prayed for help. I also prayed there would be no policemen on my path to the arena.

As we drove to the game, I know my daughters could feel my stress. I was short with them and snapped back when they were just trying to make simple conversation. I'll never forget the look in my daughter's eyes when she asked me a simple question and I answered her back in a harsh tone. I realized, in that moment, that I was the problem. I also realized that I needed to do something to change the environment, something to alter the negative energy inside that car.

What I did next was a bit unusual. I exited the highway, pulled over into the first parking lot I could find, parked the car, got out and walked about five steps away, then turned around and came back. (I know that sounds crazy!) I opened the car door, sat down, and with a huge smile on my face said, "Hey y'all, how's it going? It's good to be home!"

My daughters looked at me with "what in the world is happening here?" expressions on their faces. I could all but hear them thinking, *Who are you and where is our mother?*

Honestly, I couldn't believe what I'd just done either. I certainly had never done that before! What happened next made it all worthwhile. At that moment, and I mean *that* very moment, the atmosphere in the car completely changed. Stress completely left the vehicle. I realized I'd needed a "do-over" and that's exactly what I'd managed to accomplish. I really didn't take time to think about it, I just did it.

The truth is, I didn't like the way I was acting. I didn't like the way I was feeling. And I knew the responsibility fell on me. It's interesting that the moment I put in the effort to bring about change was the moment the whole environment around me shifted. Let's face it. We all have bad moments. We all snap back and yell and overreact. How many times have we gone to bed and thinking, *Man, I wish I wouldn't have acted that way.* If we're not careful, we can allow those ill-conceived incidents to convince us we're lousy parents or even less-than-decent humans in general. When we feel like bad people, it doesn't make for a happy environment.

Please hear me say this: *bad moments don't define us*. We have to realize that when we fail in a moment, we still have the power to fix it by choosing how we act or react in the *next* moment. Instead of making a moment into a monument and letting it continue to play on and just become worse, we can, first of all, recognize it, then take responsibility, and then change it. Mistakes are inevitable. It's what we do to correct them that really matters. We can't expect things to change for the better if we're not willing to do something that'll actually create change.

Newsflash: You are entirely up to *you*! Steve Jobs said, "Deciding what *not* to do is as important as deciding what to do." We have to choose to be disciplined about what we respond and react to. Our lives were designed to be composed of decisions, not reactions.

Simple Adjustments Can Bring Big Relief

If you know anything about me, you know I love shoes. When I see a cute pair, I can't explain it. They make my heart skip a beat. In fact,

I often design a whole outfit around what shoes I'm going to wear. Some people start from the top and move down when choosing an outfit. Me—I dress from the floor up. However, I have one rule of thumb: I never (and I mean *I never*) wear uncomfortable shoes. I spend hours standing and talking, so I can't allow what I'm wearing to become a problem or a distraction. If you ever see me in four-inch heels and wonder how I can walk in them all day, just know, they're extremely comfortable.

A while back at one of my speaking engagements, something went seriously wrong. My right shoe was hurting like crazy. I'd worn the shoes before with no problems. I couldn't figure out why, this time, the right one was absolutely killing me. I couldn't wait to get back to the hotel to take them off. When I finally got a break and had a chance to remove the shoe, I realized the strap around my ankle had flipped over. The pin on the buckle wasn't going through the hole—it was actually poking into my skin! That's what had been causing the pain all night long. I was so happy my cute little shoes didn't have to go in the give-away pile. That entire night, I'd experienced aching pain, but the reality was, I just needed to make a simple adjustment and I would've felt relief. Once I adjusted the strap, things improved almost instantly. How true is that for us in life? Some situations (I'm not implying all) could be better if we would take the time to make some simple adjustments.

Let's break this down into some easy steps.

- Don't complain (help us, Lord!), *adjust*. Let's face it, complaining is just announcing areas in our life where the enemy has been successful.
- Decide to stay calm. Remember Exodus 14:14, which reminds us that the Lord will fight for us. All mamas should take special care to listen to this one. Decide not to allow the chaos around you to override the calm within you.

- Decide that you're *not* going to be negative, even when negativity is surrounding you. Don't allow a temporary situation to cause you to turn away from a permanent promise. See, you can't always change your circumstances, but you can change your perspective.
- Don't waste your energy on things you can't control.
- Don't get involved in battles you don't belong in.

The next time you mess up and start complaining, *adjust*. Create a do-over and *choose* to stop complaining. When you slip up and temporarily focus on the negativity surrounding you instead of God's promises, practice the do-over! Shift to positive gear. When your emotions surge up to take over, demand a do-over and take control. You can actually decide to go from grumpy to happy. You can change from yelling, and possibly giving people a piece of your mind, to being calm and giving them a piece of your heart instead. You can travel from being stressed out, uptight, worried about the dishes, laundry, toys all over the ground, and a messy house to an it's-all-gonna-be-okay person. Pick what kind of human you want to be! An I-will-get-everything-back-together person? An I'm-going-to-stop-freaking-out individual? Or how about an it's-not-the-end-of-the-world-and-I'm-gonna-enjoy-this-day kind of person? Whatever you aren't changing, you're choosing. Do what you know needs to be done, even when you don't feel like doing it. If you don't like the way things are, change them to make those moments ***better than ever***. As I like to say, small tweaks lead to big peaks.

Every single day, you can do something that your future self will thank you for. Hey, life is too short to live harsh, mean, angry, bitter, unhappy, or stressed out and yelling at everyone. It's a do-over day today! Go ahead. Shock your family, spouse, friends, and co-workers. I dare you, right now, to take on the challenge of a do-over. After all, if you don't like the way today started, you can decide to start it over again.

YOUR PURSUIT

Make the conscious choice to include a do-over in a stressful moment to make this day *better than ever*.

CHAPTER 14

Fight for It

"You may have to fight a battle more than once to win it."

—MARGARET THATCHER

In 1981, my healthy, energetic mom went to the doctor because of a pain in her side. During her examination, he noticed something abnormal. He immediately admitted her into the hospital for extensive tests. Her "check-up" turned into a several-week stay in the hospital. The prognosis was shocking. The doctor told my mom and dad that she had metastatic cancer of the liver. At that time, he expressed that chemotherapy and radiation wouldn't benefit her because the cancer had spread and was too far gone to respond to any treatment. As if that information wasn't grim enough, he also added that my dear mother only had a few weeks to live.

The day Daddy brought her home from the hospital was one I'll never forget. I assure you that I certainly wasn't expecting what I saw. Mama had changed so drastically in a very short period of time. My once-healthy, forty-eight-year-old mom now looked very sick. Her skin was jaundiced, and she seemed so incredibly fragile. She weighed eighty-eight pounds and looked like she was ninety-eight years old.

If there's one word I could use to describe how she looked, it would have to be like "death." I watched as my mom and dad went into their bedroom and laid down on the floor before God. Daddy spoke God's Word over her life, saying that she would not die, but instead, she would live. He talked from his heart and in a simple, sincere plea to God said, "I need my wife and our children need their mother."

I then watched as Mama got up and placed her Bible on the floor. She slowly put her tiny feet on the Word—she physically stood upon it! Oh yes, you read that correctly. My frail and sickly mother, who'd just received a literal death decree from her doctor, actually placed her Bible on the floor of her room and stood upon it! I'd never before, and haven't since, seen such a graphic display of someone "standing on God's Word." Standing on her Bible, and with a shaky, yet bold voice, she spoke out, "Father, the only thing between me and death is Your Word…and I'm choosing to stand on Your Word."

I watched from the doorway, unnoticed by my parents. I happened to be the only child at home during this time, and I was certainly a captive audience. I was mesmerized as I stood there, silently watching and listening. I never dreamed these moments would be forever etched in my mind or that they'd have such a powerful impact on the rest of my life. To say I was amazed would be an understatement.

The next morning, I woke up and got ready for school. I can remember, like it was yesterday, the picture I saw when I walked into our kitchen. Talk about business as usual. There on the table was my hot breakfast. My sack lunch was in its usual place on the counter, just like every other school morning. Standing by the sink, washing dishes, of all things, was my little, frail mother. I couldn't believe my eyes.

"Mama, what are you doing up? You need to be in bed," I said.

She turned around and looked me right in the eyes. "April, I'm not going to lie in bed like a sick person. I believe I am healed and I'm going to act like a healed person."

At that moment Mama became my hero. As I looked into her eyes, I no longer saw death, but instead, I saw a soul surging through and through with life. Her determination to live showed me how to be a fighter—and not a lightweight, but a heavyweight. After all, she had fully grasped that this was her life the doctors were talking about. This wasn't some Bible story. It wasn't someone else. It was *her* life, and it was very real. I watched my mom shift into fighting mode. I saw her actually stand on the Word of God with a determination I'd never seen from anyone before. I heard her speak daily (many times a day), "I will live and not die, and I will tell what the Lord has done." (Psalm 118:17 ERV)

My mama was determined that she wasn't going anywhere and certainly not without a fight. And she sure wasn't about to just lay down and surrender to death. Mama had every intention of winning the battle for her life. I'm happy to say, after a year of battling and standing on the Promises of God, Mama won. She was, and remains to this day, completely cancer-free. Talk about a miracle!

I love what one of her doctors, D. L. Moore, documented: "I must tell you that knowing all the players and having seen all the tests and x-rays has made a tremendous impact on me. It is one thing to read about miracles, but it is another to sit by and watch one happen."

Harness the Determination to Never Stop Fighting

I know Mama wouldn't be here today if she hadn't decided to be a fighter. It took some bulldog tenacity, that's for sure. It took a "never-give-up spirit." It took a warrior mentality. She was in it to win it, and with God as her fighting partner, win it she did. I sometimes wonder if she realized, at the time, that she was also training up another warrior. A little warrior who desperately needed her mother. A little warrior who was praying on the sidelines, just like she'd watched her mother and father do. A little warrior who witnessed, first-hand, that God was still in the miracle-working business. You can't talk me out of miracles. I know they're real. I've seen God bring life out of what the so-called experts pronounced as dead.

I know that every story doesn't end in the same way. In fact, I'm often asked what I would've thought if Mama had lost her battle with cancer. I can only tell you this. I would still be able to say she taught me to fight and stand on God's Word. She taught me how to pray when life gets difficult, and to trust God even when life throws impossible situations your way. Her fight wouldn't have been vain. Had she chosen to gracefully check out of life and make her entry into heaven, I would've still reflected on how she never wavered on the promises of God. She truly believed then, and continues to believe today, that God is Who He says He is. He really can do what His Word says He can do.

You know as well as I do that life can fling some major curveballs at us. Bad things happen to good people. I'd add to that saying, bad things happen to good people *all the time*. Life truly isn't fair. Often, it can seem like one long, continuous battle. What I've learned is that it's really about the choices we make, in the midst of the battle, that greatly affect the outcome.

We have to choose whether or not we're going to surrender to our circumstances or if we're going to stand up and fight. May I just encourage you to be a fighter? Determine that no matter how difficult life may get, you're going to fight. Decide that no matter how many times you might fall, you'll get back up. Settle it in your heart right now that no matter how many times you might fail, you'll keep on trying. Don't ever give up! The good things in life are worth fighting for. The God things in life are worth staying in the battle for.

Focus on the One Who will get you through the battle. God always promises He will never, ever leave you. He assures you that nothing is too hard for Him. He can do what men can't do. It might be hard right now, but don't ever give up on God because He will never give up on you. When you realize this, your days can be ***better than ever***.

Always remember that our God is still, and will always be, in the miracle-working business. In case the enemy tries to convince you that the above story was a fluke, try this one on for size. When my older sister, Lisa, was born, she had something they diagnosed to be similar to cerebral palsy and brain damage. She had no sucking reflexes and no muscle tone. The doctor told my parents she'd probably be in a wheelchair all of her life. My parents, as you can imagine, were heartbroken. At the time, my dad was a pastor of a small denominational church. Up to this point, he'd never been taught about healing. Upon hearing Lisa's prognosis, my parents begin to read the Word of God like never before. They read in the Gospels about how Jesus performed miracles. Then they read in Hebrews 13:8 that Jesus was the same today as He was yesterday. My mom said they began to pray in the simplest way with these words:

> *"Jesus, Your Word says You haven't changed. Here we are faced with a little child that has cerebral palsy and brain damage. Father, if you don't change, then You are still the same now. You can touch our little girl and make her whole. Would you touch her and heal her?"*

Daily, they prayed over Lisa. That's right, they prayed over her *every single day*. They fought the discouraging thoughts that came their way, including the ones that told them their little girl would never be "normal." And then it happened. Little by little, they discovered Lisa doing things that she'd never been physically capable of doing before. Day by day, she was improving. She began to roll over, which the physicians had said she'd never do. She began to hold her bottle and drink it—another victory. It wasn't long before Lisa was completely healed. In their simplistic prayer, God heard them.

No doubt, God can turn any situation around. Let me encourage you by stating that whatever miracle you're praying for, don't give up. Keep fighting for it. Keep your faith strong. Keep your hopes high. Surround yourself with people who'll lift you up and pray for you. Keep your heart filled with expectation. Listen to things that will encourage you. Set yourself up in an environment to overcome. Watch for the victory. It may seem impossible right now, but remember, *impossible* is exactly what God specializes in.

YOUR PURSUIT

Fight for what you want, need, and believe in to make your days *better than ever*.

CHAPTER 15

Just Pull Over

"Heaven is full of answers to prayers for which no one ever bothered to ask."

—BILLY GRAHAM

Several years ago, while I was in Houston, Mama and I were in the car going out to eat. She was driving. I was talking to her when, right in the middle of my conversation, Mama interrupted me, grabbed my hand, and said, "Let's pray."

I felt the sense of urgency in her voice, so I quickly closed my eyes. She began praying for my son and daughter, Garrison and Savannah. They were traveling a four-hour drive to Houston. It was the first long-distance drive my seventeen-year-old son had ever attempted.

Mama began praying; "Lord, I thank You that angels are protecting Garrison and Savannah and they won't be in an accident. I thank You, Lord, they will arrive safely in Houston without harm."

She let go of my hand and we continued to the restaurant. Honestly, I'm so used to Mama and her praying that the incident was pretty normal for me. I tell you the truth when I say that it wasn't two minutes later that I received a call from Savannah. I asked if they were okay. She assured me they were. Then she said, "Mom, you won't believe what just happened. There was an eighteen-wheeler in front of us and he ran over a tire. That tire flew up and was heading straight for our windshield. But all of a sudden, out of nowhere, the tire dropped to the side and moved out of our way."

She finished with, "I don't even know how that happened. It was a miracle."

That story still gives me chills as I write about it. Mama's prayer wasn't accidental. It was intentional. It was done with urgency. Something inside her said, *"Pray!"* I'm so glad she did. I believe it was because of her prayer that my children's lives were spared from what could have been a tragic accident.

Prayer is incredibly powerful. Never doubt what yours can accomplish. Never doubt how important having a consistent prayer life is. The scripture says, "The effective, fervent prayer of a righteous man avails much." (James 5:16 NKJV)

Prayer is life changing. It can turn hopeless situations around in an instant. I was in Louisiana, heading to a speaking engagement. Two amazing ladies had picked me up at my hotel, and as we were driving, one of the ladies mentioned she forgot to pray over me before leaving the hotel. Before I knew it, the driver pulled off to the side of the road, put the car in park, turned around to me, and said, "Let's pray!"

Right there, on the side of the road, those ladies prayed a powerful prayer over me, the conference, and all those who would attend. No doubt, they knew the power of prayer. Sure, it could've waited until we got to the venue, but not according to them. They recognized the importance of covering someone in prayer. I was beyond grateful for their unwavering tenacity. That incident taught me that sometimes you just have to stop what you're doing, pull over, and pray. You might be in the middle of something important, but if you have that sense on the inside of you that a person or a situation needs prayer, don't wait! *Pray*! You never know what's going on in someone's life.

The scripture tells us, "The very day I call for help, the tide of battle turns." (Psalm 56:9 TLB) You never know how one prayer can turn an entire situation around.

Here's another example. One day I was sitting at the house and felt compelled to say a quick prayer for one of my daughters. I prayed a simple prayer of protection and then called her cell phone. I asked if everything was okay. She couldn't believe I called. A minute before my call, the car in front of her had stopped, suddenly, on the highway. As a result, my daughter's car hit the other vehicle...but here's the thing. Technically, she should've hit the car hard because she'd been traveling close to sixty-five miles per hour, yet, by the grace of God, her car had slowed in time to barely tap its bumper. No damage was done to either vehicle. It was truly a miracle.

Pray Like Your Kids Are Watching

Now, let's take this prayer thing to the next level. I encourage you to allow your kids to see that you're a person who prays. Invite them to listen in and even pray with you. Let them hear and actively participate in your conversations with God. Let them see firsthand how God hears and answers prayers. Let them understand how prayers and the act of praying make every day ***better than ever***.

Our kids are much like little video cameras with legs. They're taking in everything we say and do. They are seated on the front row of our lives. Why not teach them how to pray by invitation and instruction? Why not demonstrate how to live a lifestyle of prayer? When I grew up, I watched my mom pray over everything. She'd pray over parking spots, (which most always got her one near the front), the broken fridge, the washing machine, or the dishwasher. One time, our ice machine was broken. Mama prayed over that thing, and I promise you, it began working. I remember, as a kid, thinking, *I can't believe it worked on an ice machine.*

Mama's praying taught me that God was always just a prayer away. She showed me that He was involved in and cared about all of the details of our lives. He wasn't just interested in the big stuff—like the parting-of-the-sea kind of stuff—but in the little stuff too. He cared about how I was doing every day.

Well, guess what? I've been known to pray over some appliances as well. I've also enjoyed a few successful shopping excursions that were jump-started by up-front parking spots. I am happy to report, prayer has worked out pretty well for me. I guess you could say I got it from my Mama.

I'm reminded of an incident when my daughter, Savannah, was about four years old. She was sitting at the kitchen counter on a barstool, waiting for her breakfast. She wanted waffles, so being the expert chef that I am, I took the Eggo waffles out of the freezer and popped them right into the toaster. Savannah had parked herself close. She had her eye on that thing, just waiting for those homemade Eggo waffles to pop up. All of a sudden, Savannah slammed her hand down on the counter as she loudly demanded, "In the name of Jesus, *pop up*!"

I kid you not, immediately those waffles popped up and scared the fire out of Savannah. Her eyes were *huge*! I placed the waffles on her plate and turned away to do dishes. After a minute, I looked over at Savannah. She hadn't touched her waffles. Instead, she had her hand on her head and quietly said, "I can't believe it worked on waffles."

In all reality, it was probably time for the waffles to pop up anyway, but the timing of her prayer and the pop-goes-the-weasel waffles was priceless. She didn't know any better than to believe that there's power in prayer. Neither of us will ever forget that morning and the miraculous "name of Jesus, *pop up*!" waffles. For her, it was a miracle. For me, it was a reminder that one of the greatest ways my kids can learn about the power of prayer is through watching me. Our prayers matter. They have great power to make a difference. Our prayers can show those we love a lot about the amazing God that we serve.

Today, when you go about your day and God puts something on your heart to pray about, by all means, pray. Don't doubt your timing. Don't be afraid of interrupting anything in your day. Pull over and pray! Someone's life may depend on the prayer you pray. You never know what miracle can transpire because you took the time and made the effort. Never, ever doubt what one prayer can do.

YOUR PURSUIT

Pray. Prayer can make your days, and the days of those you love, *better than ever*.

CHAPTER 16

Remember Who You Are

"Life has no limitations, except the ones you make."

—LES BROWN

Years ago, our softball team was in the final game of playoffs. I was on the pitcher's mound. Whoever won the game would win the league championship. I'd already allowed two runners to get on base. The girl who stepped up to the plate looked intimidating (like maybe she might hurt me) and like she was going to knock the ball all the way into the next county. Our coach motioned for the outfield to move back—way back. Talk about pressure! The count was full, which, if you're not a baseball fan, just means that the next pitch, with the exception of a foul ball, would be the one that mattered! This batter looked like she could tear the cover off the ball with a hit to the moon so I could either walk her or (best-case scenario) strike her out. It was up to me to pitch a ball that would, hopefully, fulfill one of those goals.

Standing on the pitcher's mound was intense. I listened as the crowd cheered *her* on. Not only were they clapping for her, but they were also bringing me down by shouting out derogatory remarks in my direction!

"She can't do it!" the crowd chanted.

"Don't worry about her!" they yelled.

"You got it easy!" they shouted.

It seemed as though everyone in the stands that day was on her side. The noise around me was so great, and the negativity so strong, that I started to believe what I was hearing. My insides surrendered. My mind was racing with thoughts: *April, you can't do this. You're going to lose the game right here. The championship is all on your shoulders and sister "knock-it-out-of-the-park" is going to win the game for their side!*

Plain and simple, the pressure of the situation got to me. I'd completely tuned out of what I knew to be true. I began to focus on, or "hear," only the false truths and white noise that surrounded me. As I got into position for the next pitch, the crowd hushed. An almost eerie silence fell over the stands. Everyone was quiet, all waiting to see what would happen next. As I was focusing on the catcher, trying to get my mind back into winning the game, something caught my eye. Just above the umpire's head, behind the fence, I saw someone stand up. It was my dad. There he was, with his little 5'7" self, dressed in his baseball cap and shorts and the whitest legs you've ever seen (by which I was briefly blinded, ha!). Amid the silence and overwhelming pressure, he cupped his hands over his mouth. With all of his might, he yelled, "Come on, April. . .*you can do it*. . . . This will be the *winning* strike!"

I can't begin to tell you what that did for me. That was my dad, who I adored. The one who had endured countless hours of working with me to make sure that I was the best pitcher I could be. If anybody knew what I had in me, it was Daddy. His words of encouragement slammed the door shut on all that white noise, as well as all of the harsh words, and allowed me to find my confidence again. After all, if Daddy said I could do it, then I must be able to do it.

Well, we did it! The next pitch was indeed a strike. We won the game and the championship. What a great day that was for our team. The victory was sweet! So, what changed? Did I suddenly get superpowers and miraculously throw a strike? Of course not. I'd trained for twelve years to be the best pitcher I could be. I knew I had it in me, yet the pressure of the game pushed against me like an immovable object. It almost got the best of me. It wasn't until my dad reminded me of who I was, of what I had inside of me and what he knew I could do, that I was able to snap out of my negative attitude. Had it not happened that way, I would've most certainly led both myself and my team to defeat. Once I moved the fact that I was trained and capable into the forefront of my mind, I was able to unleash the drive and determination that'd been pushed down by all that negativity and self-doubt. My dad's words helped me get back into a mindset of victory. Isn't that how life is sometimes? Why is it that, while we know what we're capable of, in the blink of an eye, it all goes out the window? Why do we sometimes inexplicably succumb to the circumstances and conflicting voices around us?

It's because we start believing what we're *not*, instead of believing in who we *are*.

We've all gone through difficulties in life feeling alone. Sometimes it feels as though everyone is cheering for the "other" side and all the odds are against us. And if that isn't enough, the giants we find ourselves facing seem like they could be in a league of their own. Before we know it, the pressures get to us and we forget what's inside us.

In fact, the apostle Paul felt this way. In the Bible, he tells of a time when he was in Asia and didn't think he and his traveling companions were going to survive. The pressure being placed upon him was so strong that he thought his life was actually going to end. And then, in the midst of all of his turmoil, Paul reflected on the countless other times when he thought his life was over. And yet, God had always carried him through.

I can just imagine Paul talking to himself: "Come on, Paul. You got this. You can get through this. God helped you before. You came out alive. Don't worry. You're not going to crumble, and this isn't the end for you. God is on your side. You can do this thing, and listen Bubba, God did it before and you better believe He will do it again." I don't know about you, but it makes me feel a little better to know the great apostle Paul actually felt like he was going to cave under pressure!

Have you ever noticed that whenever pressure comes, it always seems like it's the first time you've ever felt that way? It's like your memory has been wiped clean of all of the other obstacles you've conquered. Negative emotions try to take us down the wrong road. Have you figured out that these emotions can discourage you and wear you out? (I've had to sort that one out many times.) But while emotions change frequently, *God never changes*. And just because we might feel like we aren't strong enough to handle a situation, that doesn't mean that God isn't strong enough to deal with anything. When we get to those places where we don't think we're going to get through, we must remind ourselves of who we are in Christ. We have to tune out the negative voices of defeat and discouragement. That's the time to think about how God has gotten us through tough times before. He will most certainly do it again. After all, He wants our days to be ***better than ever***.

There's a wonderful scripture that says, "The One who died for us...is in the presence of God at this very moment sticking up for us." (Romans 8:34 MSG) That particular verse is proof that no matter how overwhelmed, underqualified, and alone you might feel right now, God is cheering you on. What an incredible thought! Think about how amazing it is that the Creator of heaven and earth is on your side. But do you know *why*? It's because He knows what's in you. He knows what you're made of. After all, He created you in His image. That means you are not an accident; you're not a second thought, and you're not a failure. God absolutely believes in you.

When you think about it, pressure doesn't necessarily have to be a bad thing. A diamond is simply a chunk of coal that handled pressure well. The same boiling water that softens a potato also hardens an egg. It's all about what we're made of. Remember, God created us, so we know that what we're made of is solid. We also know that God is on our side, which ensures we can make it through anything.

2 Timothy 4:1 (MSG) says, "God is looking over your shoulder." In other words, God has your back. He's looking out for you. You may be facing strong opposition right now. Let me encourage you to keep the faith. The difficult times aren't the times to question God or to wonder if He's really there. Instead, they're the instances in which we say, "God, I trust in You and depend on Your faithfulness. I know You will see me through these difficult times."

Pursue Your Miracles

In the Bible (1 Kings 18:41), the prophet, Elijah, told the king, Ahab, to get prepared because there was going to be some heavy rain. Now, you have to know a little bit of the backstory here to fully understand the magnitude of this statement. Three years prior, Elijah announced to this same king that there would be a great drought in the land until he spoke otherwise. In those next few years, a lot transpired, but two things remained consistent. It didn't rain, and there was bad blood between the king and God's prophet. In fact, Elijah put his life at risk by even meeting face-to-face with King Ahab. Ahab heard what Elijah had to say...and then went on his way to eat, drink, and do whatever kings do. The scripture says that Elijah climbed to the top of the mountain and bent down to the ground. He put his face between his knees and told his servant to go look for rain. The servant came back and reported that he saw nothing. Seven times Elijah told him to go back and look. Elijah knew what he had been told by God. He knew, in his heart, that God would send the rain. Finally, the seventh time he sent his servant out, the man came back and announced, "I see a cloud as small as a man's hand is rising from the sea."

That's all Elijah needed to hear. He commanded that his servant tell ol' Ahab, "Hitch up your chariot and go down before the rain stops you." (That sounds like Texan talk!)

The story continues, telling us that the sky grew black with clouds and heavy rain began to fall. I love how Elijah knew that one teeny, tiny cloud was significant. One minuscule sign assured him his miracle was on the way. I don't know about you, but that's an attitude I'd like to adopt in my prayer life. He didn't doubt it. He didn't wait for a bigger sign or for the skies to fade to a deep, storm-cloud black. He knew that cloud, the size of a man's hand, in a great big, blue sky was confirmation of the very thing God said would happen. Elijah was consistently on the lookout for his miracle and grabbed hold of the tiniest of signs, knowing that his God could and would come through.

Let me ask you this. Are you actively in pursuit of your miracle? Are you constantly looking for it? Has God promised you something and, even today, you are still waiting for that thing to come to pass? Are you searching for your sign? When is the last time you looked for it? When is the last time you got up in the morning and said, "God, I believe my miracle is on the way. I'm actively looking for it to come forth. I know You are faithful to Your Word. I will not stop looking, believing, and staying the course in faith until I see it come to pass."

Faith is actively looking. It is proactively believing for something that doesn't seem possible in the natural, but that is entirely possible with God. Do you know your prayers are never a bother to God? Just because you don't see anything happening doesn't mean God is not working. The scripture says "it is God Who is all the while effectually at work in you..." (Philippians 2:13 AMPC)

God is working behind the scenes on your behalf. The Bible also says, "God is not like people, who lie; He is not a human who changes His mind, Whatever He promises, He does; He speaks, and it is done." (Numbers 23:19 GNT) Keep believing for your miracle. Get your hopes back up! Stand on God's Word like never before. Carry the faith in your heart that He really will do what He said He would do in your life.

One of my favorite stories in the Bible is about the prodigal son. He took his inheritance, left his family, and went to a distant country to live. He squandered his wealth and lived in a wild way. Finally, when he had come to the end of his money, he got himself a job feeding pigs and was so hungry he wanted to eat the pig's food! That's when the Bible says that the son finally came to his senses. He realized, in the midst of starving, that he would do better as one of his father's servants back home. He knew he had messed up so badly that he could longer be considered a son but believed that maybe his father would hire him to work in the fields. He figured at least then he wouldn't starve to death.

Now comes the part I love. Luke 15:20 says that while he was still a long way off, his father saw him and was filled with compassion for him; he ran to his son, threw his arms around him, and kissed him. Even while the son was telling his father he knew that he was no longer worthy to be called "son," the father was wrapping his best robe around him, putting a ring on his finger, sandals on his feet (see, shoes are biblical!), and was even planning a feast. He was celebrating that his son, who was once dead, was now alive again.

I can just imagine that father getting up every day, looking out his front door, hoping beyond hope that he would see his son. I can picture him every time he's out in the field, looking over the horizon for his boy's return. I can only imagine how when he went into town, he was combing the crowds, looking for a glimpse of the one he loved. He certainly wasn't giving up. Instead, he chose to continue to hope, pray, and watch for his son's return. He had made up his mind that he was going to keep looking until he saw what he wanted to see.

I don't know what kind of miracle you need today, but I want to encourage you to actively pursue it. God really does care about what you're facing. He hasn't gone on vacation. He certainly hasn't forgotten about you. The Bible says the very day we pray, the tide of the battle is turning. (Psalm 56:9) You're stronger than what you're going through, so don't give up just because it's tough. Don't quit because things might appear to be getting worse.

Let me assure you, God hears and answers prayers. God is for you, so don't allow *you* to be against you. Don't allow the process to discourage you either. Don't allow the bad news and setbacks to put you in a tailspin. Don't allow what you see to cause you to forget what God has already said. Look at your situation with eyes of faith. Don't focus on the problem. Focus on the promise. Keep believing for those kids. Keep trusting God to do a miracle in your marriage. Keep waiting for the spouse God has for you. Keep believing for a miracle in your health. Keep standing on what God has declared over your life. You do what you can do, and then watch what God will do! If God said it, He will do it. If He spoke it, it will come to pass. Take it from me, a bigger, stronger person standing on the "mound" of life isn't going to keep your miracle away. Believe in yourself. Believe in God. At just the right time, He will make it happen. Remember, the tough and challenging times are when God sees what you've done with what He made you out of.

Think about it like this: tough times are training times. God wants you to get to the place where you focus on the Mountain-Mover and not the mountain. He wants you to tune out the naysayers and "turn up" what His Word is saying. Don't let what you're currently facing paralyze you. You may feel like the Apostle Paul—that your situation is going to get the best of you. Give it to God and trust that He will work everything out. Circumstances surrounding you might be convincing you that there's no way out, but God wants to remind you He can do "exceedingly abundantly above all that we ask or think." (Ephesians 3:20 NKJV) It may not feel like it, but with each battle, you can become stronger. Don't back down. Instead, choose to fight back, because with God on your side, you've got this! Maybe you're feeling the pressure right now. You're on that pitcher's mound of life. Hey, it's okay. Take a deep breath. Stop telling yourself you can't do it. Now, look beyond what's staring you in the face. A little bit higher. Ahhh...there He is. Listen closely and I think you might hear Him saying, "Come on! You can do it! This is the strike that's going to bring you the victory!"

YOUR PURSUIT

Remind yourself that God made you and is there for you. With Him on your side, your days can be *better than ever*.

CHAPTER 17

Get Out of Your Own Way

"Success is the ability to go from one failure to another with no loss of enthusiasm."

—WINSTON CHURCHILL

One night, after wrangling all of the kids into bed, I went downstairs and turned on the television to relax. I kid you not, it must have been "female preacher" night. It seemed like every channel I turned to was airing another wonderful woman giving a vibrant message about God. On one channel, this beautiful lady was preaching up a storm, quoting scriptures, one after another. She was so good. I watched with admiration at how effortless she made her dynamic presentation appear. I turned the channel afterwards, only to find another. This woman did things a bit differently by preaching a bit and then singing while accompanied by a beautifully played organ. She was amazing too! I enjoyed her, but after a while, I found yet another channel. You guessed it. Still another fabulous female preacher. Not only could this one preach heaven down, but she had these great theatrical hand movements! I have to tell you, I was mesmerized. After enjoying Fancy Hands for a while, I changed the channel one last time and finished off my viewing time with one of my all-time favorite people, Joyce Meyer.

Now, you'd think all of these amazing women, clearly anointed by God, would've filled my heart with joy and left me encouraged and ready to take on the world. Well, you'd be wrong. The truth is, I couldn't watch any more. My discouragement became so great that I actually turned the television off. After seeing all of those fireball preachers, I began to think about everything I wasn't.

I can't preach like her.

I can't carry a tune in a bucket.

I'll never be as knowledgeable as Joyce Meyer, and I certainly don't have any fun hand movements.

As I sat there drowning in my own self-pity, a devastating thought occurred to me: *I probably don't help anyone when I preach at the services.*

This new idea dancing around in my head was a huge deal, especially because at that time, I was an actual pastor at a church in Texas. Can you imagine being a pastor who feels like she can't preach? It was disheartening to say the least. Every service, I'd get up and do my best to share an encouraging word with our congregation. I loved speaking life and hope every week. It was my sweet spot, and honestly, I thought I was halfway good at it...at least until that night. I went to bed thinking that the next day, which of course was Sunday, would probably be the last time that I'd ever get up on stage at our church and encourage people the way I'd done for years and years.

Well, we had three services that morning. I did my thing in each service, feeling like I wasn't really making any type of impact. During the last service, I tried to add in some hand movements and almost dropped my microphone. I was embarrassed and even more discouraged—if that was even possible. At the end of my last message that morning, I sat down in my chair, humiliated and resigned to the fact that I'd probably never be on that stage again.

As the service continued, the entire congregation, me included, stood to sing a song. A lady came up to me very unexpectedly, which was startling. I tried to be cool, but then, she very loudly declared, "April, God wanted me to tell you that you don't have to be like anybody you see on TV!"

I about fell over as I thought, *Lord have mercy. Was this woman in my house last night*?

She quickly added, "God wants you to know you don't have to be like anyone else, except the person He has designed *you* to be!"

Well, I have to tell you, in that moment, my discouragement exited stage left. Once I stopped being against myself, I began to embrace who God created me to be. I stopped thinking in terms of my being a non-singing, non-hand waving, definitely non-Joyce-Meyer-type preacher. Instead, I realized that God had created me to minister in my own unique way. I don't have to be like anyone else. I just get to be me.

I wonder how many people are aware that the enemy rarely misses an opportunity to discourage us. He doesn't want us to see our value or to know our worth. He wants to distract us by inviting us to focus on everything we're not, so he can keep us from everything God has promised we are.

Stop the Dollar Store Mentality

My youngest daughter, Arriella, and I went to the store to get some gift bags for Christmas presents one year. We tried a store we'd never shopped in before. It was close to the house. We started loading up the basket with bags. What was strange was that none of the bags had prices on them. I looked all over for a price tag but couldn't find even one on anything. Arriella came over with a handful of bags and let me know she couldn't find prices either. It was so weird.

Finally, I decided to go find a sales associate and ask. I mean, we were buying a lot of bags. Just as I was about to ask, I looked up. All around the perimeter of that store were signs that read: Everything Is a Dollar!

Arriella saw the signs as well. We looked at each other and said, "There is *no way*! How in the world could everything be a dollar?" Y'all, we'd wandered into The *Dollar* Store. We had no idea the store name actually meant that everything literally cost one dollar!

I looked inside of our shopping cart and started pulling out bags. I took out a small bag, thinking, *Maybe this could be a dollar, but not this big bag…it's way too big. There's no way these two bags can be the same price. That's impossible.* In essence, I was wanting to pay more because I had concluded that a bigger bag should cost more. I was actually trying to rationalize away an amazing bargain!

I wonder how many times we carry a "dollar store" mentality when we remember what God has said about our lives, and the destinies He has always had lined up for us? How many of you have had thoughts like this:

God, I know You said this, but, man, that promise couldn't possibly be for me because of all I've done.

You couldn't possibly use me in a way similar to how you used her.

I'm not qualified. I've failed too many times.

I know you originally had a great plan for my life, but now I understand if it's less. Because I'm so flawed.

Can I tell you some really, really great news? God doesn't pick people the way people pick people. (Say that ten times!) His love is unconditional. He loves you despite your mistakes or how many times you've failed in the past. He's loved you throughout your imperfect history. When you make Jesus the Lord of your life, He wipes the slate clean and will never bring it up again. Not only that,

He has an amazing future in store for you, not based on your performance, but on His promises. That, my friend, is an amazing Savior.

What am I getting at? It's simple: Don't allow your imperfections, your shortcomings, or your flaws that no one knows about keep you from all that God has in store for your life. Remember, we're all a work in progress. Don't talk yourself out of your destiny because of preconceived ideas you have about your life. Don't settle—get out of your own way!

Only Dust Should Settle

Did you know that we weren't created to simply settle in life? God designed us for lives of abundance. He wants us to overflow with peace, joy, happiness, and everything else that goes into great living. He wants us to succeed and fulfill all of our dreams, the dreams that He placed inside our hearts. He wants our days to be ***better than ever***.

Aren't you glad that your God isn't a "barely get by, barely making it, family on the verge of falling apart, marriage in crisis, job in jeopardy, hardly enough money to live" kind of God? We can be thankful that He isn't like that. God doesn't want us to resign ourselves to something less than or to settle for anything other than abundant and extraordinary. If we know He feels that way, then the question becomes: Why would we ever want to disagree?

Refusing to settle applies to many different areas of our lives. Whether it's an unfulfilling job, relationship, home life, or other pursuit, every day brings the opportunity to change the circumstances. How you define that "change" is personal and unique to you, but all transformation is only possible by putting forth the effort, energy, and grace. Here are some examples:

- **Work Life**: Don't settle by staying in a job where you aren't satisfied or that doesn't fulfill you. No, I'm not suggesting that you quit your job today. I'm talking about working toward your dream job, so you can move into a better tomorrow. Do you want to be a writer? Wake up a few hours earlier every day and work on your project before you go to work. Do you desire your own business? Use your free time to gain experience and begin to network. Whatever your dream job is, begin to find small ways to bring it to pass. Consider doing things that are out of the ordinary to get you to the place you desire to be. You'll know when the time is right to step into that life where you get to wake up each morning excited, filled with desire and passion, eager to work toward the things that God has placed in your heart. It won't happen overnight, but if you stay disciplined and determined it'll happen.

- **Marriage**: Don't settle for a marriage that's only so-so—a marriage you'd define as barely making it. Do what you can to make your marriage flourish. Attend marriage seminars. Read books that can help you both. Do whatever it takes for you and your spouse to get on the same page and on the road to a thriving relationship. Don't keep living the same way, complaining about everything that your marriage is not. Don't settle. Do something, every single day, to make your marriage everything you want it to be.
- **Home Life**: Don't settle for a home that is filled with strife and arguing, and where the normal is yelling and chaos. Sit down for family dinners. Turn the phones off and have conversations. You simply have to be more involved in your kids' lives. Set the tone for peace. Be a builder of hope, love, and mercy, but at the same time, be the parent. Your kids don't need more best friends. Put your foot down when you need to, set the boundaries, and say "no" when necessary. Remember, it's not about being popular, it's about being the

parent. Make the necessary changes that you need to have an enjoyable home life with your amazing family. Remember, amazing doesn't just happen. You have to work toward it.

- **Self-Talk**: Don't settle in your mind. Say no to those thoughts telling you that you can't, or won't, or that you'll never be able to do this or that. Clear out the thoughts echoing that you're not good enough, smart enough, or talented enough. Clear the clutter in your mind. Say no to fear. Hey! You might be afraid. And that's okay. We're all afraid at times, but don't let that hold you back. Don't let fear dictate your life, and certainly don't let it cause you to settle. Do it afraid! Whatever it is! Step out beyond the fear with a faith that says, "I can do all things through Christ who strengthens me." (Philippians 4:13 NKJV)

Let me encourage you. God is for you, so don't spend any more time settling or being against yourself. Stop beating yourself up. Stop looking at your flaws and inabilities. Stop comparing yourself to others and realize you're valuable just as you are. Know that God has a purpose for your life.

After reflecting on these facts, isn't it time to get out of your own way? You may not be where you want to be right now, but thank God that you're not where you used to be. Your life isn't about who others say you are. It's about who God says you are. In God's eyes, you're beautiful. You're truly one of a kind. You're His masterpiece. Never forget that you're special, loved, chosen, and forgiven...and you're family. You aren't your sin. You aren't your failure. You aren't your mistakes, and you're certainly not your past. Here's a piece of invaluable advice: Stop reminding God of what He has already forgotten. Leave the past in the past and move on.

One day, a farmer was looking at his crops, when all of a sudden, he heard a horrible scream. He ran to see where the noise was coming from, only to discover that his sweet little donkey had fallen into a dry well. This donkey and farmer had been together for years. He loved that donkey. The farmer worked and worked, doing all he could to get the donkey out of the well, but to no avail. He had nothing that could reach far enough down into the well to pull the donkey out. As sad as he was, the farmer didn't want his donkey to suffer long, so he went and got his shovel. He began to shovel dirt down onto the donkey.

When that first bit of dirt hit the donkey, the poor creature freaked out. But after a few shovels of dirt landed on top of him, he shook really hard, knocking the dirt off and onto the floor of the well. Every time the farmer threw a shovelful of dirt onto his back, the donkey would shake it off, again and again. The more dirt that was thrown down the well by the farmer, the higher the ground rose. After about an hour, that little donkey stepped out of the well and licked his master's face, happy to be safe and secure again. What seemed like total defeat actually turned out to benefit the donkey. Why? Because of the way he handled the adversity thrown his way.

Whatever has been holding you back, whether it is feelings of failure, your past, or anything else, shake it off and invite each and every day to be ***better than ever***. Use your obstacles as a stepping-stone toward your God-given destiny. Embrace who God has made *you* to be. Do what you can with the talents you have. Use the time you have in a positive way. Don't leave your dreams and gifts on the table. That's settling. Let go of who you think you need to be and step into the person God created you to be. If you think about it, life is too short to be anyone else.

YOUR PURSUIT

Focus on your victories and what makes you special. If some area of your life needs work, don't settle. Remember that God wants the best for you, so put in the time and effort and watch your days become *better than ever*.

CHAPTER 18

Stay Balanced

"Life is like riding a bicycle. To keep your balance, you must keep moving."

—ALBERT EINSTEIN

When I was about ten years old, I decided I'd ride my bike to my friend's house a few blocks away. On our street, the houses were situated on large, acre-sized lots. All of the neighbors had dogs that would usually hang out in their respective front yards. Most of the dogs were allowed to roam freely since they were friendly. They never really bothered us neighborhood kids.

However, there was one canine that, well, let's just say, didn't get the friendship memo. His name was Vonston. He was really mean, so he had to be chained up in his yard. He barked at everyone who rode, walked, drove, or just thought about going by his property. Even though he looked and sounded ferocious, I never worried much about ol' Vonston. I guess I just believed in my heart that those chains protected me.

On this particular day, I was riding down the street, and good ol' Vonston barked at me as usual. As I pedaled, his barks seemed to be growing louder and louder, which seemed a little odd. Even still, I didn't think too much of it—that is, until I felt something by my right leg. I looked down and couldn't believe it! It was Vonston! Somehow, he'd managed to get himself free and was keeping pace with my bike, trying to eat me. His teeth were big and sharp and actually really white. My little ten-year-old legs pedaled faster than they'd ever pedaled before. I never knew what the name "Vonston" meant, but that moment cemented my personal definition: "demon dog from the pit of Hades."

As if being stalked by Vonston wasn't traumatic enough, the nice, usually friendly, neighborhood dogs decided to get in on the chase. At one point, I looked back and saw eight dogs chasing me. Yes, I said *eight*! Somewhere from the depths of my young soul, I found more pedaling power and I pushed ahead while desperately trying to keep my balance. I pedaled and Vonston panted, his stubby legs running at top speed. It was like a bad, bad dream.

My family had no idea I was outside, fighting to get away with all my limbs intact. Somehow, some way, but by the grace of God Almighty in Heaven, I actually made it to my best friend's house. I got off my bike at the stop sign and looked back to see Vonston and those dogs watching me. Then they walked nonchalantly back to their little houses, without any display of guilt or shame for scaring me half to death. As my breathing returned to normal, a sense of relief started to wash over me. I'd survived. (Cue: "Survivor," by Destiny's Child.) I'd out-biked the crazy, evil dog gang and made it through without as much as a scratch.

My friend and I ended up having a great time at her house, which made me forget about the demonic dog gang...at least until I got back on my bike to head home. Getting home required me to bike back down the same street where I had nearly become dog food a few hours earlier. Honestly, I wasn't sure I had it in me to do it all over again. And the reality was, I didn't even want to try.

But I did try, and I did make it home. I guess the dogs were exhausted from their earlier jaunt and decided to leave me alone. I felt a sense of pride when I got to my front door because I didn't let those dogs deter me from my playtime.

Now I when I think about that day outriding Vonston and crew, I realize it's a perfect metaphor for life. Let's face it. Life can get tiring. It can be hard, complicated, and overwhelming. One day, you're out minding your own business, enjoying a nice sunny afternoon bike ride, when *boom!* all of a sudden, a "Vonston" crisis hits and we find ourselves faced with decisions that could have major repercussions. Then, just when we've made it through one thing, *boom!* something else happens. More difficulties and even greater challenges arise. We suffer losses, experience trials, go through valleys, face mountains, and sometimes, quite frankly, it seems like all we do is continually fight to get through the current crisis at hand. Life pulls at us from all directions. If we're not careful, we can lose our sense of direction, our balance, and even our desire to do what we set out to do in the first place.

But guess what? We have to keep pedaling. God didn't promise a life that would be a bed of roses. He did, however, promise He would be with us through the trials and challenging times. He encourages us to give our worries and concerns over to Him. He doesn't want us to go through life weary and worn out, but instead, live a life of abundance in every area. The Bible shows us that His desire is for us to "prosper in every way and be in good health physically just as [we] are spiritually." (3 John 1:2 HCSB)

God wants us to live a balanced life. Scripture also says: "Be well balanced (temperate, sober of mind), be vigilant *and* cautious at all times; for that enemy of yours, the devil, roams around like a lion... seeking someone to seize upon *and* devour." (1 Peter 5:8 AMPC)

We have to be aware that the enemy wants to catch us off guard, then come in and steal our joy...which in turn, steals our strength. When we get out of balance, it opens the door to fatigue, worry, unhappiness, and so much more. An unbalanced life is an unhealthy life. When we become stressed, overwhelmed, and overworked, these conditions not only negatively affect us, but everyone around us as well. In these situations, it's difficult, if not impossible, to have days that are ***better than ever***.

Listen, I know life has a way of pulling us in a hundred directions. I have five kids! I also know we have to fight to do our parts to keep life as balanced as we can. Notice, I said we have to *fight*. A lot of times, it's a daily battle to manage everything thrown at us.

One night, I was sitting in my car at a red light. Next to me was a large truck that looked pretty impressive from my vantage point. On the side was a banner that advertised that the truck was a work vehicle for a tool company, promising tools that could repair anything. Now, I'm not much into tools or big trucks, but with my background in marketing, I have to say this truck's graphics had me convinced they were the ones to call when I needed repair work done in my home. Then, as the truck began to pull away, my view completely changed. As the truck gained speed and progressed down the road, I could see that the entire truck looked like it might fall apart at any second. If, in fact, their tools could fix anything, then someone needed to apply them to the truck. That vehicle was shaking from front to back, making the most horrible noises. It looked like an accident waiting to happen. I even chose to speed up and pass the vehicle, just to get clear in case anything happened to fall out or off of the rig.

How often do you find yourself in this same condition? Okay, I'm not saying you're an old truck, but you know what I mean. It's easy to get wrapped up in the message we want to send, in the look of our life, in the graphics of us. Sometimes, though, we fail to see we could use a tune-up, recharge, or maybe even a complete overhaul. We can make ourselves look good on the outside, but what's happening within may be a very different story. The scripture tells us, "[Our] bodies are temples of the Holy Spirit." (1 Corinthians 6:19 NIV) In other words, God has given us this body that we live in to take care of and treat right. He wants us to have high standards for our temple, His home. After all, this is the only body we have in this lifetime.

Choose Good Habits

For most, a healthy, balanced lifestyle isn't just going to "happen." It's a choice we have to make. We can either continue with the same course of bad habits and bad health choices or decide, today, to make a lifestyle change. If we don't take time for our wellness, we'll be forced to make time for our illnesses. That's a powerful statement and a wakeup call for all of us.

The key to keeping your balance is knowing when you've lost it. What we do at the tipping point makes the difference. Allow me to express a few ideas concerning health and wellness.

Stop wearing yourself out and stretching yourself too thin. Yes, I'm talking to you! Think of all of the activities you're involved in. Are they stressing you out? Are you running all over creation on Saturdays for the sake of your kids? Is your schedule causing you to be overwhelmed? Then reassess your life. Sit down and figure out what you can do that won't bring stress, but instead will bring joy and allow room for flexibility.

I've had to do this many, many times. With my kids, my travel, and work, I often have to sit down, reset, readjust, refocus, and restart. Complaining about it won't do a thing. Life won't change unless you do something to change it.

Get some rest. (Somebody just said *amen*!) So many of us are running on such few hours of sleep. Get in a routine. Start going to bed at the same time every night. This will make you feel better, and it reduces anxiety and stress. Adequate sleep increases clarity, focus, happiness, and inner ease. Do you want more balance? Get some sleep!

Eat for longevity. You are what you eat, so don't eat cheap, easy, or fake! Eat your veggies and fruits, and drink lots of water. (Do I sound like your mom?) Say no to processed foods and soda. Limit your sugar. Feed yourself like someone valuable. Nourish to flourish!

Rethink who's around you. If certain people are sucking the life out of you and causing you to be out of balance, then readjust. If you allow people to make more withdrawals than deposits in your life, you'll be out of balance. Catering to others unnecessarily will put you in the negative. Maybe it's time to close the account on some relationships.

The bottom line is: you can't serve from an empty vessel. Become a priority in your life and take care of yourself! Your health and well-being should be an investment and not an expense. And believe me, one of the wisest investments you can make is in yourself. Don't continue to go through life only wishing things were different. Stop making excuses and begin making changes. You can do it! Do it for you. Do it for your family. Life has no remote control. You have to get up and change your channel yourself! It's time to chain "Vonston" back up. Get back on that bike and enjoy your life.

YOUR PURSUIT

Take action to live healthier and with a greater sense of your own balance and value. Realize your body and soul are important to God and know that He wants your days to be *better than ever*.

CHAPTER 19

Be Your Biggest Fan

"You have to believe in yourself when no one else does."

—SERENA WILLIAMS

A few years ago, I received a call for what sounded like an amazing opportunity. I was invited to be an inspirational speaker for a success seminar that would travel around the United States. The event was centered around something that I'd never done before and encompassed a completely different audience than what I was used to. As our conversations progressed and they explained my role in more detail, the job continued to sound wonderful. The more they talked, the more excited I got.

But even in the midst of my excitement, my internal voices were haunting me with negative talk.

You know you can't do this, April.

You know you've never done anything like this before.

April, you're just a preacher's kid who grew up and became a preacher girl.

You speak in churches, not on world stages.

And so on, and so on. I had seriously conflicting messages ricocheting between my heart and mind. While my heart was excited and passionate about everything they were telling me, my mind had already decided. *Not qualified. Thank you, but no thank you.*

At the end of a fairly long conversation, they asked me if I would like to join the team. I kid you not, my mind said *no*. But for some reason, the word *yes* came out of my mouth. Even as I continued listening to them unpack their vision for the success seminar, I thought, *What did I just agree to? Why did I just say yes?* I wanted to take it back, but I couldn't.

When I hung up, I thought, *Dear Lord, what in the world did I just agree to?* My heart sank down to my feet. I knew my crowd and what they were all about. Well, this wouldn't be my crowd. I'd never done anything even close to this before, and let me tell you, I was terrified.

In all the drama of the moment, I happened to remember that, just a few weeks earlier, I'd prayed and asked God to open new doors in my life. I'd implored Him to take me to places that I'd never been before. I petitioned Him to help me meet the right people, people who could provide me with new opportunities. I had to smile when I realized He had done just that. Here was my new opportunity, complete with new places and a new crowd. It was staring me right in the face.

If I'd prayed for this and it showed up, then wouldn't I need to give it a try? With these thoughts in mind, I hesitantly began to prepare for my new adventure. What's interesting is once I gave in and began preparing, things started to unfold nicely. Consequently, I began to feel, on the inside, that maybe, just maybe, I could do the job. I wrote down my ideas, then turned them into a twenty-five-minute inspirational message. I started getting really excited once again. That's not to say I wasn't still nervous about the whole thing. I can assure you that I was. I had a ton of questions going through my mind. *Will they like me? Am I going to be a good fit? Can I really do this thing?*

But when these queries would overwhelm me, I went on the defense. I began to say to myself things like:

April, you can do this. You got this.
You were made for this moment.

This crowd needs to hear what you have to say because your message is filled with hope. It's going to bring life and healing to all who hear it.

You have what it takes. You are bold. You are strong.
You are gifted in what God has called you to do.

Now, please don't let anyone ever tell you that positive affirmations are a waste of time. They aren't. Every single day, I'd cheer myself on. You know why? Because I needed the encouragement. I needed someone to believe in me and I discovered that person could (and should) be *me*! I knew my words had to be stronger than any fear that was trying to keep me from all that God had in store for me in this new opportunity.

Even when I spoke at the first event (and actually while I was speaking), I continued being my own cheerleader. *You've got this, April. They're taking it all in. They're going to leave as better people because of the message you're sending their way. They're going to love you. They're going to want you to come back.* Yes, I was mentally cheering myself on, even while I was speaking. In effect, I was cheering confidence in and fear out!

Guess what? Each time I spoke, it got easier. I became more and more comfortable. Not only that—I absolutely loved what I was doing. For the next ten months, I traveled all over the United States and Canada doing the very thing I didn't think I could do. I'm so thankful that I didn't allow fear to hold me back from a new chapter unfolding in my life.

Sometimes, we just have to become our own cheerleaders! We don't always have to look for encouragement, because let's face it: it won't always be there. We don't need a fan club or cheering section. We have *us*! The scripture even tells us that, "David encouraged himself in the Lord!" (1 Samuel 30:6 KJV)

Speak *Life* into the Environment

It's okay to become your own number-one supporter. After all, if you don't believe in you, how can you expect others to do the same? World-class big-wave surfer Laird Hamilton said, "Make sure your worst enemy doesn't live between your own two ears." Are you constantly saying, "I can't do it," "I'll never make it through," or "I don't have what it takes?" Guess what? You can't and you don't. You see, more times than not, we become exactly what we choose to believe. Henry Ford was spot-on when he said, "Whether you think you can or think you can't—you're right." We prepare for interviews, speeches, and important conversations, but seldom ever think about the conversations we have with ourselves.

What are you saying to yourself? Are you building yourself up or are you tearing yourself down? The Bible says, "Words kill, words give life; they're either poison or fruit—you choose." (Proverbs 18:21 MSG) This is a powerful verse. You need to make sure you are speaking "life" into your environment.

We have to realize that if words can create trouble, then they can create transformation. If words can create doubt, then they can create belief. If words can create negativity, then they can bring about the positive. My dad used to say, "Don't use your words to describe your situation, use your words to change your situation." How we talk to ourselves really does matter.

We can talk ourselves into defeat or we can talk ourselves into *victory*.

We can talk ourselves into a frenzy or we can talk ourselves into *peace*.

We can talk ourselves into staying right where we are, or we can talk ourselves into our *destiny*.

Don't tell yourself every reason you can fail. Speak to yourself like you're a champion, a winner, and someone who will exceed expectations, and watch your days become ***better than ever***. You have to speak faith into your world, even during the hardest times of life.

When my mom was sick with cancer, she had a vision of health. It was contrary to how she looked and most certainly how she felt. She had to make an effort, in the worst time of her life, to remember what it was like to be healthy. She did something that I'll never forget. She found pictures of when she was healthy, happy, and strong and put them all over the house. She was setting herself up for victory. Everywhere she went, throughout our home, all during each day, she saw pictures of strong, healthy, happy, healed Dodie. She had to keep a vision of victory before her eyes. She'd also speak her vision out loud: "Father, I thank you I'm healed. I'm healthy. I'm strong. I will live and not die and proclaim the works of the Lord." (Taken from Psalm 118:17 KJV)

Mama knew the words she spoke became the house she lived in and what shaped her world. In the midst of the worst, she chose to make her words work *for* her and not against her. You can't talk defeat and expect victory. You can't constantly talk about your problems and expect a solution. If you don't speak positively over your life, who will? If you don't have anything positive to say over your life, then don't say anything at all! The scripture says, "Keep your mouth closed and you'll stay out of trouble." (Proverbs 21:23 TLB)

Keep your mouth closed when you want to criticize yourself. Keep it closed when you're feeling defeated. Keep it closed when what you're going to say isn't going to encourage and cheer you on towards your dreams. Remember, it takes two years to learn to start talking, but a lifetime to learn when to stop. One Bible verse says, "... an encouraging word cheers a person up." (Proverbs 12:25 NLT) In other words, become your biggest fan. Clap for yourself! Give yourself a pep talk! You are going to do amazing things! Always know that with God on your side, you have the majority.

YOUR PURSUIT

Be aware of negative self-talk. Transform your word choices so you speak kindly to yourself and about yourself, and feel your days become *better than ever*.

CHAPTER 20

Spread Your Wings

"The secret of change is to focus all of your energy, not on fighting the old, but on building the new."

—SOCRATES

There are occurrences that take place where you can remember everything that happened like it was yesterday. These are the most monumental of moments that make a long-lasting impact. For me and my family, one of those events happened in 1999 when my father passed away. He'd been sick for a little while, but honestly, I didn't realize things had progressed to the point where he would die. It came as a shock to all of us.

Almost instantly after his death, it was announced on the news. There was a particular reporter who decided to give the statistics of the likelihood of the church surviving if either a son or daughter took over. He said that any efforts would fail. This was not the news we needed in the middle of a devastating situation. I have to tell you, it was hard. My dad had pastored the church for over forty years. The weight of how we were going to fill his shoes was almost too much for my mind to conceive. I didn't know how it was going to work. On top of everything else, I was about two weeks away from delivering my fourth baby. My dad had been there for the birth of all of my other kids. I couldn't fathom him not seeing our new baby girl.

Even though we didn't have it all figured out, God did. He showed up in a big way. The process of moving on without our dad was difficult and challenging because we were all stepping up and doing things we hadn't done before. We were being stretched far outside of our comfort zone. But God was always there, leading us every step of the way.

My brother, Joel, became pastor of the church, which is a story in itself. Until he stepped in, he was behind the scenes, never out on the platform. You better believe it was a miracle when he got up and started speaking. The first time he preached, I was sitting in my seat sweating because I wanted him to do great. And he did. He and my family have continued to soar to new heights, reaching people we never even dreamed possible. Once we spread our wings, we began to soar.

Certainty Often Comes from Chaos

We all know change isn't easy, but it's going to happen. You may not like it, but sooner or later you're going to be faced with situations that will pull you out of your comfort zone. Situations that challenge you to grow and stretch beyond your limits are inevitable. You can either be open to the change and growth or you can shrink back and remain the same. John Maxwell said, "Change is inevitable, growth is optional."

If you're not willing to change, your life won't change either. I hesitate to think what would have happened if we'd crumbled under pressure after my dad's death. Things certainly wouldn't have turned out the way they are now. We could've missed out on the next thing God wanted to do with the church and within each of our lives. Sometimes, our lives have to be shaken up to get us to the place we are destined to be. It's often in the chaos and uncertainty of our lives that we find our direction.

A few months after the transition of the church, our little family had it in our hearts to move to the Dallas area and start a church. We'd trained under my parents and felt it was time, so our little family packed up and set out on our new endeavor. Now, you have to understand, this was a stretch for me. I'd never started a church before. I'd been in our family's church all of my life. I knew we were supposed to go, but I have to tell you, the fear was there. The change was hard for me! I had to decide whether or not I wanted to step into something new, out of my comfort zone, or remain within the safety of my world.

I decided I didn't want to remain the same. With my car loaded with our four kids (at the time), ages seven, five, three, and ten months, I made the four-hour drive to Dallas. Almost the entire way, my mind was in overdrive with questions.

How do you start a church?
How do you get people to come?
How do you get money to start a church?
Where do you start a church?

I was overwhelmed with my lack of answers. I remember the exact place on the highway where I said out loud, "God, I don't know how to do it, but I'm giving all of my questions, all of my uncertainties, and all of my fears to You. I know this is what we are supposed to do, and I'm just going to trust that You are going to help us and lead us every step of the way."

I felt like a load was lifted. I chose to stop thinking of all I was giving up and began to look at everything I'd gain. I had to create a mindset shift. And to be honest with you, I had to choose a mindset shift daily, sometimes several times a day. Why? Because change isn't easy! I had to trust that God was with us and that He was going to take care of us. I trusted Him to ease my mind. The scripture says, "Leave all your cares and anxieties at the feet of the Lord, and measureless grace will strengthen you." (Psalm 55:22 TPT)

Let me tell you something. I needed that grace. As we set up our new lives in Dallas, we discovered things about ourselves that we didn't even know were in us. We had some amazing people come into our lives who walked alongside us as we began our new adventure. We started from the ground up, with fifteen people in our living room. Eight of those people were kids! We would've counted dogs if we had them. We worked together as a family. After filling up a high school auditorium three times on Sunday morning, we bought a beautiful campus that housed our sanctuary, as well as an accredited private school that we started. All of the kids attended. We were living our dream. We pastored that church for fourteen years. I have to tell you that I loved that church. I loved those people. They were a part of me. They brought such joy to my life. Through the struggles, the mistakes, the good times, and the bad, I wouldn't change it for the world. Who would've known that out of the loss of my father, something amazing would be birthed?

There's something magical about new beginnings. Oh sure, the ending of the previous season might be hard. It might even be the hardest thing you've ever had to go through. But if you trust the process, you'll see the new doors that open, the new beginnings, the new opportunities that arise. So, are you going to step forward into something new and different, or are you going to remain safe? If your life was exactly the way it is today in ten years, would you be happy? If not, then maybe it's time to get out of your comfort zone. Maybe it's time to stop being scared of change. Maybe it's time to stop thinking of all of the reasons it won't work and stop focusing on everything you have to give up. Trust that God will help you through the process.

What if change brings you closer to your destiny? What if change means progress? What if a door closing means a new one is about to open, ushering in opportunities to make your life ***better than***

ever? What if an ending simply means a new beginning is around the corner? When I look back on that drive from Houston to Dallas when I was so filled with fear, I'm so glad I took the leap of faith. Because this one thing I know: God was faithful every step of the way. In fact, that struggle made me stronger. Amazingly, the next time I was faced with change, it was a little bit easier to conquer.

You might feel a change coming right now. Don't fight it. You may not have it all figured out, but God does. He's not worried. He's not in heaven biting His fingernails and hoping it all works out. He believes in you. Now it's time to trust He will take care of you. Each time you conquer change, it becomes a little easier the next time you face it. It might be the hardest thing you've done so far, but it might also be the right thing. Don't be afraid to start over. Don't be afraid to step out in faith. God has never left you before. He's not about to do it now. You've got this. You can do it. You are strong. Just when the caterpillar thought the struggle was too strong and her life was over, she spread her wings as a butterfly and began to fly. And guess what? It just might be the time for you to spread your wings too.

YOUR PURSUIT

**Open your heart and mind to change.
Trust in God and let Him be your guide so you can move in the direction of living *better than ever*.**

CHAPTER 21

Start with the Heart

"Knowing what you need to do to improve your life takes wisdom. Pushing yourself to do it takes courage."

—MEL ROBBINS

Several years ago, I developed a bump on my middle finger. I didn't think too much about it, other than it slightly hurt and was very unattractive. I covered it with a Band-Aid on most days so it wouldn't be visible. This one particular day, I was walking with my mom and she looked at the Band-Aid and asked what was wrong with my hand.

"I don't know," I said, "but it's been there for quite some time."

My mom looked closely. She then said the worst thing ever: "It's a wart!"

I nearly fainted. I didn't want to have a wart. Even the name "wart" is yucky! (If you have a wart, I'm sorry. I'm sure it's fine.) You better believe I went to the drugstore as fast as I could and bought every product that had the words "wart" and "removal" on the packaging. I'm sure I tried every one of those products. I put ointment on it. I prayed over it. I put even more (or maybe a slightly different) ointment on that ugly little wart. Had I any access to some holy water, I would have sprinkled that on it too. I promise, every time I prayed over it, I felt like that obnoxious wart multiplied! It was getting bad, fast. (Don't worry, I'll never, ever pray for you if you have warts.)

At one point, I had twenty-three warts on my finger! I know... *yuck*! I'm kind of grossed out right now just telling you the story! If that's not enough, in time, I developed warts on the thumb of my other hand. And yet, there's more. Y'all, I looked down on my leg and there they were ten warts setting up residence! I didn't even know you could get warts on your leg. I couldn't believe this was happening. (Okay, stay with me. It'll eventually get better, I promise.)

Any time I ventured out in public, including to attend church, I concealed my growing population of warts. On one particular Sunday we were blessed with a guest speaker, an amazing lady named Marilyn Hickey, who I've known since I was a little girl. My oldest daughter, Christiana, and I were sitting in the front row enjoying the message when (and I'm not joking) she went over to the side of the podium, leaned against it, and said, "You know, God has really given me an anointing to pray for people with tumors and warts. And I'm just going to ask right now in the middle of my message, if you have a tumor or a wart, please stand up and I'm going to pray over you."

I kid you not! My heart began to pound. I began to sweat. I thought, *She is so talking to me and I am so not standing up*! There was no way on God's green earth that I was going to let the whole congregation in on the fact that I was slowly being taken over by a wart demon! I'm supposed to be Warrior Chick, not Wart Chick!

As she talked, one side of my mind was screaming for me to stand up while the other said no way. Finally, I thought, *Come on, April. What have you got to lose? You've tried everything and nothing has worked.* So, I did it. I slowly stood up, feeling like I weighed about two thousand pounds. I was so embarrassed. I felt like a spotlight was on me with a big "Hi, I'm April and I'm covered in warts" sign hanging over my head. I was hoping the congregation thought I had tumors. Lord have mercy. What in the world was I thinking?

As she was getting ready to pray, she said, "I want you to touch the part of your body that is affected and then we will pray."

I'm thinking, *Dear God in heaven, are you kidding me? What is* not *affected?* I nonchalantly folded my hands together, secretly touching my thumb and bandaged finger. Then I thought, *I have to get my leg in on this prayer.* So, I leaned down and acted like I was scratching my leg, looking all contorted. Y'all, I was beyond embarrassed.

She finished the prayer. I have to say, being the spiritual person that I am, that I've never been so glad for a prayer to end in all my life. I just wanted to sit down, curl up, and die.

"Well, that was embarrassing," my daughter said as soon as I took my seat.

Thank you for those extremely life-giving words of encouragement. Geez! I wish I could tell you that, miraculously, the next morning all of the warts had disappeared, but they hadn't. Weeks went by, and instead of them going away, I'm pretty sure a few more popped up. Finally, I got frustrated. I let God in on my feelings.

"God, I don't know what else to do," I said. "I've tried everything I know to do to get rid of these ugly things. I've prayed and the warts have multiplied. I stood up in front of our congregation. I was humiliated and embarrassed for everyone to see how flawed I am. And even Marilyn Hickey prayed, and nothing happened. God, what is going on?"

I'll never forget that, in the stillness and quietness of my frustration, I know I heard God say in a gentle, yet firm way, "April, how can you expect to help others, when you don't even have the guts to admit you need help yourself?"

Boom. I don't know if you've ever been corrected by God, but I sure was that day. I was knocked down to where I needed to be. You see, I was embarrassed to show people my imperfections. I didn't want them to see how flawed I really was. The reality was that I needed to get my pride out into the open. I had to let go of the thought that I had to always "appear" like I had it all together, that my prayers always get answered, that life is good, and blah, blah, blah, blah, blah.

I needed to embrace the fact that it was okay to be the perfectly imperfect me who had struggles just like everyone else.

I realized I was praying for God to change my circumstances when, all the while, God was wanting first to change me. God brought me to the place where I needed to be. For that, I'll be forever grateful. It wasn't easy, but it was well worth it. It's a lesson that has stayed with me throughout the years. Now, instead of praying, "God, please change my circumstance," I first say, "God, if there's anything in me that you need me to work on, show me. God, change me."

The scripture says it clearly: "Create in me a clean heart, O God, and renew a right spirit within me." (Psalm 51:10 ESV) When we get the inside right, it's a whole lot easier to get the outside right. I'm also happy to say, in the end, I won the battle of warts. Over the next few weeks, they slowly started disappearing, and it wasn't long after that moment of clarity that they all disappeared. No more Band-Aids, no more hiding—just imperfect me doing life, one day at a time.

Victory Happens on God's Timeline

God is just as concerned about who we're becoming as He is about where we're going. He will use every adversity, challenge, and hard situation we face to bring us to a new level. He does this because He knows that every "next level" of our lives requires a different us. In other words, the very thing we might be fighting against could be the thing we need to master before being promoted to the next level.

My battle wasn't with warts. It was the *pride* on the inside of me. You might be facing something difficult right now. Maybe in the middle of it all, God is trying to do some things in you. I'm not saying He sends disease or difficulties—I'm saying there are things we can learn in the center of these trials.

When life puts the squeeze on, something is going to come out. That's when we discover things about ourselves that we probably didn't even know were inside us. Maybe some doubt needs to go, maybe procrastination, or maybe God is trying to show us not to drag our feet and ignore doing the thing He wants us to do. Maybe there's some pride that we need to get rid of.

All I know is something is going to change in the midst of the storm, and if you allow it, it can be you. There's a story in the Bible about a highly respected commander of the Syrian army named Naaman. Naaman had leprosy and was told to go see a prophet named Elisha so he could be healed. Naaman went to the prophet's house and, the truth is, it didn't go well. Instead of Elisha coming down to pray over him, he sent his servant to tell Naaman to go wash seven times in the Jordan River. The servant assured him that if he did this, his leprosy would be gone. (2 Kings 5:9–10 NET)

Now, Naaman was kind of a big deal. He didn't appreciate the prophet not coming down himself. The scripture goes on to say, "...I thought for sure he would come out, stand there, invoke the name of the Lord his God, wave his hand over the area, and cure the skin disease." (2 Kings 5:11 NET) Well, as a result of being snubbed, Naaman was not a happy camper, to say the least. And the fact that Elisha sent his servant to tell him to go dip, of all places, in the Jordan River, the filthiest river out there, well, it just added insult to injury. And because Naaman didn't like the way this situation was being handled, he got offended. The Bible says, "So he turned around and went away angry."

Thank God for Naaman's servants, because they told him, "Come on, man! Who cares if the river is dirty? Just jump in and be healed." (Obviously, that was my interpretation of the scripture.) Well, Naaman finally got over himself. He went to the river, dipped seven times, and guess what? He was completely healed. But Naaman almost missed his miracle because of his pride. He almost walked away, allowing his anger and offense to rob him of his healing.

Imagine if those servants would've gotten offended by Naaman's bad attitude and all walked away angry? Thank God the servants knew better and instead told Naaman what he needed to hear. It was simple, yet profound. It brought him to the place he needed to be.

I want to encourage you now to check your heart. In fact, check it often. Don't ever allow anger and offense to be the roadblocks that keep you from your miracle. Let God do His perfect work on the inside of you. Trust His ways and His timing. Trust what He tells you to do. Victory always comes through God's plan of deliverance and not necessarily through our version of how things should happen. Be open to Him doing a little open-heart surgery on you. Trust me. When He does, your life will be ***better than ever***.

YOUR PURSUIT

Pay attention to how pride may be holding you back. Open up your heart to hear what God has to say and follow His words to make your life *better than ever*.

CHAPTER 22

Train the Quit Out of You

"I never tried quitting, and I never quit trying."

—DOLLY PARTON

Years ago, I was having a routine checkup for my third pregnancy. I was forty weeks in, and to me that meant I had another week before the baby would even think about coming into this world. My first two kids had been at least a week late, so I wasn't overly concerned. I figured this one would most likely follow suit. My regular doctor was out of town, so I saw the doctor who was taking his place that week. He told me everything was fine, no signs of the baby coming any time soon, and I was good to go back home. As I was leaving the office, I had this sudden, strong, overwhelming feeling that I needed to have the doctor take another look. Despite it being beyond obvious that I wasn't anywhere near having the baby, I couldn't shake my unsettled feeling.

You can imagine how awkward I felt going back upstairs and telling the doctor that I'd like him to please recheck me. I'm not going to lie. He looked at me like I was just a tad bit crazy. Thankfully, even though he was unconvinced, he did as I asked. Much to both of our surprise, he told me I was indeed in labor. I needed to go to the hospital right away. The interesting thing is, I had no contractions, pain, or feelings associated with labor at all. And hey, I know what it's like. Like I said, this was my third kid! By now, I was kind of feeling like a professional at the baby thing! Even though I didn't feel like I was in labor, the doctor and I walked next door to the hospital to check in.

After the nurse confirmed the vital signs of both me and the baby, she told me to lay back and rest. It would be a while before this little one made her grand entrance into the world. She left the room and I still wasn't feeling a thing. Then, about a minute later, my water broke. As you might imagine, the pain was intense. The baby was on her way. The nurse came back in and saw that the baby was on her way out, ready or not! The two words that came out of her mouth remain something that no pregnant woman on the verge of delivering a baby ever wants to hear: "Don't push!"

The room wasn't ready for delivery. Well, I could see that, but you have to understand that at this point, I was in some serious pain! I completely believe in supernatural childbirth, and it's spelled E-P-I-D-U-R-A-L. Because the baby was coming so fast, I couldn't get my supernatural epidural, so this mama was feeling pain like I had never felt before. Let me tell you, this mama needed her drugs!

The room was chaotic with people preparing to do what they do so well. I was on the bed, and I actually thought, *I don't want to do this right now. This is too painful. This hurts too bad. I just want to go home and take a nice, long, hot bath and go to bed. I'll deal with this another day.*

As if I had a choice! In the middle of those crazy thoughts, I bet you can figure out what happened. The baby came within a few minutes. She was healthy and strong, and the joy of seeing our newest family addition completely wiped away the pain of her delivery. But can you believe in the middle of delivery I wanted to quit? I actually wanted to go home and deal with the pressure later! Isn't that how our minds work sometimes? The pain, pressure, and struggle of our daily lives sometimes seems so great that, instead of getting through the process, we attempt to "opt out" and try, instead, to run, or at least fast walk, away from facing a situation at all. And all the while what's being birthed is right around the corner.

The greatest reward any woman could ever have only comes after she endures some of the most intense pain imaginable. I'll never forget what I heard a minister say to me one time: "April, there's no progress without the process." In other words, sometimes you gotta go through some not-so-good things to get to the desired outcome. You could say we have to go through it to get to it. And guess what? Quitting won't speed up the process.

Scripture tells us the temptations in our lives are no different from what others experience. "And God is faithful. He will not allow the temptation to be more than you can stand. When you are tempted, He will show you a way out so that you can endure." (1 Corinthians 10:13 NLT) It may be difficult. It may be excruciating. We may be looking for the epidural of life and not having any luck finding it. Just hang on.

Trust that God is with you and that He's going to help you make it through. Don't allow the enemy to convince you to quit. Train the quit right out of you! The prophet, Elijah, had seen miracle after miracle. He prophesied there'd be no rain, and there wasn't for three years. Then he prophesied the rain was coming again, and it did. He was fed by ravens when he was hungry. He saw God multiply flour and oil. He witnessed a widow's son raised from the dead. He called fire down from heaven in the battle of the gods and the prophets of Baal. You know, just everyday things that we all face. But after managing all of these great feats, we find Elijah in quite the predicament. He was running from King Ahab's wife, Jezebel, because she was out to end his life. She was so angry that Elijah killed all the prophets of Baal that she said, "May the gods strike me and even kill me if by this time tomorrow I have not killed you just as you killed them." (1 Kings 19:2 NLT)

Those words got under Elijah's skin. Shocking, but true. He became afraid of this woman. So, he did what any solid, proven in the spiritual battle world, true man of God would do. He ran for his life! He went into the wilderness all alone, sat down under a tree, and actually told God to take his life. It's like all the great things he'd witnessed and been a part of instantly vanished from his mind. Elijah then fell asleep. (I'm not sure I would've been able to sleep under similar circumstances, but that's just me.) At any rate, right in the middle of his nap, an angel woke him up and told him to get up and get something to eat. (Now that's my kind of angel!) Elijah glanced around and noticed that right next to him was warm baked bread and a jar of water. He ate, drank, and then went back to sleep. Then the angel came back, woke him up again, and told him to get up and eat some more, because he was about to go on a long journey. He needed to be fueled up. Elijah ate and drank again, found a cave, and spent the night.

While he was in the cave asleep, God woke him up with a whisper and said, "What are you doing here, Elijah?"

Elijah responded, "I have zealously served the Lord God Almighty. But the people of Israel have broken their covenant with you, torn down your altars, and killed every one of your prophets. I am the only one left, and now they are trying to kill me, too."

This great man of God found himself isolated, worn out, exhausted, and ready to end his own life. God could've said to him something like, "Come on, man. Quit having a pity party and acting like you're the only one who's ever done anything risky or hard and get back to work!"

But He didn't. When God saw that His servant had no energy and no fight left in him, that he was burnt out and just wanted to quit, God said, "It's ok, Elijah. Jezzie is not gonna get ya. Have a snack, get some rest, and then let's carry on and, as always, I'll continue to be right here, walking beside you. I have so much more in store for your life." (This may be my interpretation of the conversation!)

The point is that when Elijah had a time of rest and refreshment, he gained a whole new outlook on life. He no longer wanted to quit, but instead got back in the game and continued with what God had called him to do.

Rest Replaces Quit

I think it's safe to say we all have had times when we wanted to quit. You're tired. You're worn out. You feel like you're doing everything possible and getting zero help. If you're not careful, those feelings can turn into burnout and lead you to a place of isolation. And trust me, isolation is never good. It gets you alone with yourself, and that's a foolproof way for you to truly start believing the lies of the enemy, the discouraging thoughts, doubts, and other half-truths that he tries to imbed into your brain. You may find yourself saying things like:

> ***"God, I'm the only one. I can't do this anymore."***
> ***"I'm tired of the struggle."***
> ***"I'm tired of the pressure."***
> ***"I don't think I can take this anymore."***

Thoughts like these are a slippery slope to a downward spiral that can lead any of us right directly into the place God found and rescued Elijah from. The place where he truly wanted to quit everything and was so depressed that he wanted to end his own life. While *isolation* is defined as getting alone with yourself, *solitude* means getting alone with God. There's a big difference. When Elijah was alone with himself, his circumstances were magnified. Suddenly, this Jezebel situation became so big in his eyes that he wanted to punch his own ticket to the afterlife. This is proof that if we're not careful, one person can drive us away from our destiny—or worse, can even drive us into feeling unworthy.

One of the most expensive things we can ever do is pay attention to the wrong people. Elijah was tormented by this devious woman's words. And because he was tired, run down, and feeling scared and intimidated, he got caught up in the emotion of the moment. And everything went downhill from there.

While emotions can make us want to quit, we have to remember that emotions come and go. Feelings are temporary. Don't put your feelings in charge of your life. Sometimes, what you need is some rest. Some good food. And a cupcake. Okay, I added that last one for free. Take care of yourself. Slow down. Be still and rest. God even tells us to take a day off where we're not thinking about work, but instead, enjoying the day. Get your mind clear and relax. Allow your body time to recharge. If you get tired, learn to rest, not quit. The temptation to quit will be at its most convincing and forceful right before you're about to succeed. Like I said, train the quit out of yourself. Keep going. Keep pushing. There are amazing things right up ahead to make your life ***better than ever***.

YOUR PURSUIT

Take time to rest. God wants us to be still and recharged so we can tackle obstacles, overcome difficulties, and make our lives *better than ever*.

CHAPTER 23

Look Beyond the Wall

"It's not what you look at that matters, it's what you see."

—HENRY DAVID THOREAU

I was a wide-eyed five-year-old kid who just loved sitting in the front row of Daddy's church. You'd find me there every Sunday morning and Wednesday evening, and often even Thursday or Friday night as well. The church was our life. I grew up in it and I absolutely loved it.

Sunday after Sunday, after we finished singing our hymns, Daddy would get up on the platform and, as a prelude to his message, ask us all to turn to our left and look at the wall. A wall with absolutely nothing on it. Of course, we all did as he instructed. (Just imagine an entire church full of people looking at the same wall!) He'd continue by saying, "Now I want you to look beyond the wall with your eyes of faith and see a five-thousand-seat auditorium. See it filled with people. See the crowds coming to every service. See people getting free from things that have held them captive. See those who haven't been loved receiving love. Look out and see the altar filled with people turning their lives around and receiving the hope of eternal life. Now let's put our faith together and pray."

At that time, our church seated a few hundred people, but Daddy knew there was much more around the corner. As much as I can remember, this happened at the start of every service, and I thought it was normal. While I didn't know what a five-thousand-seat auditorium looked like, I knew it was bigger than the one we sat in. My little five-year-old mind saw a giant church, filled with people who were happy, singing, coming to the altar, receiving prayer, and getting healed. As God would have it, I can tell you that it wasn't long before we had that five-thousand-seat auditorium. And as I sat in the front row of the new church building, guess what I saw? A church filled with thousands of people singing and happy to be together. I saw people coming to the altar and getting healed. I watched, during each service, as individuals came from all walks of life to find hope, love, freedom, and eternal life. It was just like we had prayed it to be.

Beyond that proverbial wall of faith was our miracle, just waiting for us to walk into it. My dad had no idea what he was teaching me every Sunday, but he was showing me to believe in God for big things. He was showing me to stand in faith for things that, at the time, might even seem ridiculous. He showed me how to talk about it and to see it through my eyes of faith. I learned to look for what I was believing for every day, to prepare for it and speak as if the thing I was praying for was real and in the process of being delivered. Daddy taught me not to focus on what was staring me in the face, but to always look beyond it.

There's something greater beyond the wall, but you have to believe that. You have to live as if you know it's there. So often, we focus on the obstacle that's staring at us in the face. We may only see the difficulty, but God only sees destiny. He wants us to put our faith into action and not be distracted by what things may look like. Ask yourself what's on the other side of the wall, just waiting for you to show up...just waiting to make your life ***better than ever***.

Do you see brokenness in your family and marriage, or can you look beyond the wall and see your family unified and happy? Can you see your marriage restored and thriving, better than it has ever been?

Do you see yourself continually struggling financially, barely able to get by? Or can you look beyond the wall and see yourself living in abundance, not lacking for anything, and being able to provide for yourself and your family?

Do you see yourself unhealthy and sick? Or can you look beyond the wall and see yourself in the best shape you've ever been in, super healthy and strong?

What you see matters.

You have to get to the place where you can see what's on the other side. The scripture says, to "write the vision, and make it plain on tablets, that he who reads it may run." (Habakkuk 2:2 MEV) Place your vision inside your heart. Write it down. Look at it every day. Know where you want to go. And then run with it until you see it come to pass.

Every year, my brothers and sisters and I get a text from our mom that tells us what she is believing for our families for the new year. Here's an example of one of them:

> *I trust you and your families will be blessed, especially this year. I pray that your children will be blessed and excel in all that they undertake to do. That we will all be healthy and well and that God will protect us and watch over us in all we do. I pray there will be no accidents or harm and that we will use wisdom in our everyday lives. I pray that our churches will be blessed and that hurting, unloved, sinful people will come in the doors and feel love and give their hearts to Jesus. I pray that drug addicts, former prisoners, and prostitutes will come and feel love and forgiveness. I pray that the anointing of God will be upon our lives, that we will be quick to forgive and forget and not hold grudges. I pray that*

every one of us will be a good parent and that our children will feel secure in their homes and that they will have good memories of their childhood and lives. And I pray, above all, that people will love us and respect us and that we will be like Jesus, with a magnificent reputation. I love you and I am blessed to have you as my child. Mama

I love how Mama is so specific when she prays. She has no shame in writing down the details. She paints the vision so clearly that we know exactly what it is she is talking to God about on behalf of her children. With this action, Mama is seeing beyond the wall.

You Become What You Believe

The scripture says that when blind men came to Jesus for healing, Jesus first questioned them, asking, "Do you really believe I can do this?" Their response was a resounding yes! Then Jesus spoke: "Become what you believe." And instantly the two men were healed. (Matthew 9:27–31 MSG)

We would all do well to commit Jesus's words to memory:

"Become what you believe."

Put this command on a sticky note on your bathroom mirror or the refrigerator, or wherever it can be seen daily. It's also important that we have a vision of *what* we're believing for and that we're clear and specific. I love how Daddy was specific with his vision. He painted a picture so vividly that a five-year-old could understand it. When you make the vision crystal clear and begin to see it through your eyes of faith, it builds a growing level of excitement on the inside of you. When you're excited, you begin to talk about what you believe will come to pass, and an act of verbalizing and visualizing helps you believe it even more. When you buy into something, that inner excitement churns. Why? Because the words you're speaking are framing your world. Your words color your environment, in the same way that my daddy's words colored that small church building.

In the same regard, you could choose to continually speak the opposite, uttering things like:

"This will never happen."
"I'm not good enough."
"They'll never choose me for that promotion."
"My idea will never come to pass."

And on and on. Guess what happens next? These negative words will probably be what *will* end up happening. You'll live in a "house" of discouragement and hopelessness. Please remember that the words you speak not only color your world, but they also become the environment you inhabit.

There was a young man who grew up on a dairy farm in North Carolina. His dream was to become a baseball player; however, when he accepted Jesus at seventeen, he felt that God was calling him to preach. The first three times he preached, his palms were sweaty and his knees were shaking. His message, each time, was pretty much a disaster. On his fourth try, he ran out of words after eight minutes. He sat down, confused and embarrassed. He told God that he didn't want to preach anymore. Besides, even if for some unearthly reason he ever did want to risk this embarrassment and humiliation again, he truly couldn't imagine anyone ever allowing him another chance.

Luckily for all of us, the desire to preach that was buried deep in his soul just wouldn't leave him. He finally relented, telling the Lord, "If you want me, you've got me."

Needless to say, no one was knocking down his door to ask him to preach again. Among other things, he'd been told that he waved his arms too much and that he was way too loud. On top of that, he was also made to feel bad because of his thick southern accent. But, even though the odds were against him, he prayed and practiced in private. He knew, in his heart of hearts, that he was called to preach. He didn't let the lack of invitations to speak stop him. If no one would come to him, he decided that he'd have to go to them. He preached on the street corners and in front of bars. He was slugged by a barkeeper, thrown off the streets by a gang, laughed at, and even booed, but through all of that, he kept on preaching.

Eventually, churches began to issue invitations. He held tent meetings. The crowds began to grow. He started traveling around the world and ended up preaching to millions. By the time it was all said and done, this man had a front-row seat to watch millions of people become saved. Billy Graham (that's right, Reverend Billy Graham) had to look beyond the wall of his limitations to see what God would and could do with a southern boy who made a decision to keep going until his dream was realized. And after that shaky start, Billy Graham became one of the greatest evangelists of all time.

I've said it before, and I'll repeat it here: It's not about how you start—it's how you finish. Begin looking at your life differently today. Look beyond the tears and envision joy. Look beyond the failures and see how God is a God of new beginnings. Look beyond the fear of the unknown and see that God has it all figured out. There's life beyond the wall.

Practice seeing through the eyes of faith. Don't speak about what you currently see, but instead, speak life into what you *want* to see. When you change what you're saying, you'll change what you're seeing. Get a vision of abundance in your life. Get a vision of health and healing. Get a vision of unity for your family. Get the vision of a thriving business. Get the vision of that new house. Get the vision of college paid off. Get the vision to make your life ***better than ever***. Become what you believe, because what you believe, you build. What you doubt, you delay. Don't look at what's staring you in the face. Look beyond the wall. There are amazing things up ahead.

YOUR PURSUIT

**Start crafting your life beyond the wall.
As you articulate your vision, be specific and be focused,
and watch your life become *better than ever*.**

CHAPTER 24

Forgive, Then Forgive Again

"To forgive is to set a prisoner free and discover that the prisoner was you."

—CORRIE TEN BOOM

If I could tell you about something that reduced negativity in your life, would you be interested? How about something that lowers your heart rate and blood pressure, reduces stress, helps you sleep better, and ensures you'll feel amazingly better overall? What if I could promise that if you master this one thing, you'll have a better today and a brighter future? Surely you'd want to know more, right? Well, I'm here to tell you the answer is right in front of you.

It's called *forgiveness*.

I know, I know. You were hoping it was chocolate and new shoes. (Hey, that works for me!) I think one of the greatest acts of forgiveness was demonstrated by the late, great Corrie ten Boom. In his book, *Seven Women: And the Secret of Their Greatness*, Eric Metaxas writes that Corrie and her sister, Betsie, were arrested for hiding Dutch Jews from the Nazis in their home in Holland. They were taken to Ravensbrück, a concentration camp in Germany. The two sisters stayed together until Betsie lost her life a few months later.

Metaxas writes that after Corrie was released from the camp, she was determined to tell people all over the world about the saving grace of Jesus, and that's exactly what she did. But one morning in 1947, while speaking in a church in Munich, she was faced with something that challenged her faith immensely. After speaking a message on forgiveness, Corrie was approached by a man. As he came closer, she recognized him. Immediately, Corrie had flashbacks to the horrible room with a "pile of dresses and shoes in the center of the floor." She remembered the huge spotlights that shone brightly as she and all of the others had to walk naked in front of authorities. Her mind rewound right back to the horrible concentration camp where she lost her sister. This is because the man approaching her was one of the cruelest authorities from the camp. As he reached out his hand to shake hers, Corrie froze, hoping he didn't remember her. Metaxas writes:

> *"A fine message, Fraulein!" the man said. "How good it is to know that, as you say, all our sins are at the bottom of the sea!"*

The man goes on to say, "You mentioned Ravensbrück in your talk. I was a guard there.... But since that time, I have become a Christian. I know that God has forgiven me for the cruel things I did there, but I would like to hear it from your lips as well. Fraulein, will you forgive me?"

Corrie stared at him, emotions swirling. How could she forgive this man? How could she forgive the detestable things he had done? She struggled with her thoughts. How could God allow her to be put in this position with this horrible man?

As she wrestled with how to answer, Metaxas writes that Corrie reminded herself that forgiveness is an act of the will, and not an emotion. She cried out to God for help. Then, hesitantly and reluctantly, she extended her hand and thrust it into his. As soon as she did, a warmth covered her body and tears began to flow. That day,

Corrie was able to forgive the man who'd caused so much pain and heartache in her life.

Corrie lived as she spoke, and is quoted as saying: "Forgiveness is the key that unlocks the door of resentment and the handcuffs of hatred. It is a power that breaks the chains of bitterness and the shackles of selfishness. Forgiveness is not an emotion. Forgiveness is an act of the will, and the will can function regardless of the temperature of the heart."

What an amazing story of the power of forgiveness. Every single day, we're faced with opportunities to be offended and hurt. It's what we do with those feelings that sets the tone for our lives. Let's face it. We have to get good at forgiving because it's something we'll have to face for the rest of our lives. Dr. Martin Luther King Jr. said it best: "Forgiveness is not an occasional act. It is a constant attitude."

Don't Let Anger Steal Your Joy

On the flip side, unforgiveness causes you to dwell on the past. It takes you back to moments of pain. It can lead to bitterness and anger, and hold you captive to a moment, whether you realize it or not. When you aren't forgiving someone, you have a definitive situation in your mind that you keep rehearsing like it happened yesterday. You can easily recall specifics about the day, the place, and even what that person was wearing. Every time you tap into that feeling, the freshly painted scenario pops up in your mind, causing you not only to relive it, but to feel those same emotions. Lack of forgiveness steals your present happiness, and if you don't let it go, it will steal your future joy.

Unforgiveness often leads to bitterness. Bitterness is the result of holding on to negative experiences. You can't expect your life to be sweet if you're bitter. The only solution is to forgive. The scripture says, "Be kind and compassionate to one another, forgiving each other, just as in Christ God forgave you." (Ephesians 4:32 NIV)

Aren't you grateful that God didn't wait for us to say we were sorry before He sent His only Son to die on a cross for the forgiveness of our sins? Aren't you so grateful that when Jesus forgives us of our sins, He removes them "as far as the east is from the west"? (Psalm 103:12 NIRV) And not only that, He doesn't remember them anymore! He's blotted them out. He has erased them from His memory! In other words, He is never going to throw your mistakes back into your face. Ever. Period.

God wants us to live a lifestyle of forgiveness. And sure, we aren't as good as Him in this whole forgiveness thing, but we can learn to forgive. While forgiveness doesn't change what happened, it changes how we feel about what happened. It releases us from carrying poison around on the inside. Forgiving doesn't mean that we always forget; it just means we don't remember with anger.

Forgiveness doesn't mean you are saying, "I approve of what you did." It means you rise above it. The act of forgiveness doesn't make them right. It simply sets us free. Forgiveness creates a new way to remember. It changes our perspective on life. Forgiveness doesn't make us weak. It means we're strong enough to know that people make mistakes. For example, when our spouse messes up, that attitude of forgiveness helps us to remember all of the good things, instead of focusing on what they've done wrong. It gives them grace and mercy. A forgiving attitude doesn't allow a mistake to ruin something beautiful.

Perhaps, you've heard the saying, "We are very good lawyers for our own mistakes, but very good judges for the mistakes of others." Walking in forgiveness also means giving grace, even if people don't deserve it, when they don't say they're sorry, and even when they don't think they're wrong. You'll never forgive if you are waiting to "feel" like it. You just have to decide to do it. No one can make you forgive. You have to find it within yourself.

An evangelist said something derogatory about my dad on television and it made me mad. The Sunday after it was said, Daddy got up in front of the church and mentioned this man's name. I was sitting in my seat thinking, *Oh good, he's gonna get back at him and set the record straight.*

Can you believe I was thinking that?

But Daddy simply said, "Let's join hands and pray for so-and-so."

I was thinking, *You have got to be kidding. He lied about you. And you want to pray for him? What in the world?!* But my dad prayed a great prayer over that evil evangelist, I mean evangelist. He didn't refer to the incident at all. It was a genuine, heartfelt kind of prayer that I didn't think the man deserved. But I learned a great lesson that day. I mean a for-real, carry-it-into-adulthood, change-my-perspective-on-life kind of lesson. Daddy taught me how to deal with people who aren't kind; people who just do you wrong. My dad showed me that two wrongs don't make a right, even when you've been treated unfairly. I learned that God is our vindicator. I learned to take the high road, keep a clear conscience, and to speak well of others. Better yet, if you don't have anything good to say, then just don't say anything at all.

It's almost impossible to hate someone who you're praying for. We can't allow other people's actions to take away our peace. I'm grateful for that valuable lesson because it made my life ***better than ever***. If we hold a grudge, we can also teach our children to hold a grudge. If we don't forgive, we're teaching our children that unforgiveness is right and justified. If we're constantly talking about how bad "they" are and rehearse, out loud, what "they" did to us, we're inviting our kids to join in on our offenses.

Some people carry other people's offenses simply because they're conditioned to do so. Instead, teach your children that there's freedom in forgiveness. Show them how to let it go. Don't let what happened to you take away your happiness any longer. Stop keeping records and start losing count. Stop allowing what hurt you to keep haunting you. Make the decision today that you're going to leave the past in the past and move forward. Do it for you. Do it for your family. Do it for your future.

YOUR PURSUIT

Practice forgiveness. Recognize that forgiving is a choice and make it happen. When you forgive easily, your life becomes *better than ever*.

CHAPTER 25

Master Peace

"Peace is its own reward."

—MAHATMA GANDHI

I'll never forget the year my kids decided to sign me up for their school "feast" without asking me first. And I'll never forget how they also thought it would be a good idea to tell me about the event two days before it was to happen. Now, of course, I'm up for doing my part. Always. But this was absurd. Two nights before the event, I was lovingly informed that I was to bring the school two turkeys, as well as corn, salad, sweet potato casserole, green bean casserole, bread, dessert, paper goods, and drinks. And, oh yeah, the news kept getting better: the amount of food needed to be enough to feed about forty people!

And, as if that wasn't enough, on that date, I was scheduled to go out of town for a speaking engagement. My goodness! You better believe my mind was flooded with questions. *How can I possibly get all of this done? When am I going to have time to study? Why did I have so many kids?* Okay, just kidding on that last one. But seriously, to say I was stressed beyond words wouldn't be overly dramatic. The good news? I got it all done. I made it to my event. Thanks to Honey

Baked Ham and the "meal to feed a multitude" service available for pick up that morning, the "feast" was a rousing success.

I'd imagine that a lot of you have your own "feast" story. Maybe not specifically finding out you need to feed an army in less than forty-eight hours, but something that completely overwhelmed you. As we all know very well, life gets quite hectic, and it's easy to lose both our minds and our peace. If we're not careful, we might find ourselves dreading everything instead of enjoying anything. Dread is sneaky. We might become victims and not even realize it.

Let me give you some examples. We dread when our babies are young, because we don't get any sleep. We dread the toddler years, and the teenage years. We dread paying for college and weddings. We dread getting up early, going to work, and getting older. We dread phone calls, checking emails, and paying bills. We dread going to see our families for the holidays, including the cooking, cleaning, and company. And the list goes on and on and on.

The point is dread causes worry and worry takes away our peace. Worry assumes the worst. Worry is the interest paid in advance on a debt we might never owe. Worry takes away today's peace. It never changes the outcome, but it does change us. It causes us to become frustrated, irritable, grouchy, grumpy, negative, nervous, fearful, doubtful, anxious, concerned, and uneasy. Author Corrie ten Boom said, "Worrying is carrying tomorrow's load with today's strength. It is moving into tomorrow ahead of time. Worrying doesn't empty tomorrow of its sorrow, it empties today of its strength."

Isn't that the truth?

My daughter Elliana had to take a routine hearing test because she works around airplanes. She was in the testing booth and, as instructed, would raise her hand when she heard the high-frequency beeps. All was going well until she didn't hear anything at all for about a minute. Instantly, she began to worry that she had lost her hearing. Her heart was racing as she prepared for the worst possible news. The instructor came to the booth and said, "I'm sorry.

The test ended a minute ago. I forgot to tell you it was over." In Ellie's mind, she'd already worked out the worst-case scenario, only to be told that the test was over. There had been a sound reason why she stopped hearing the little beeps.

God wants us to participate in a lifestyle of peace. He will never use fear to guide us. He is the God of peace. He will never use anxiety either. The scripture says He leaves us "with a gift—peace of mind and heart." (John 14:27 NLT) He desires that we stay in that peace and not in stress. Peace is maintaining an inner calm, while walking in the midst of the everyday storms that are blown our way.

I was sitting on a plane in Dallas, waiting for it to take off from the airport. I had a speaking engagement the next day and was eager to get to my destination. Everyone had boarded the plane, but no one had shut the door yet. Needless to say, nothing happens on an airplane until that door is shut and locked. Consequently, I could only interpret this to mean one thing. My flight would most likely be delayed. Sure enough, after a short while, the captain's voice came over the loudspeaker and informed us there was a "mechanical issue." These are two words you're always happier to hear while on the ground!

At any rate, the captain said he didn't think it would take long to repair the issues and asked us to sit tight, promising he would keep us updated. I don't know about you, but I'm perfectly fine waiting for a mechanical issue to be fixed before we take off. In fact, I would even be completely okay with changing planes. I'm all about everything going smoothly.

After a little while longer, sitting in the crowded, stuffy airplane, the guy sitting a few rows back began to loudly voice his complaints about the situation. He didn't just want the plane to take off, he wanted it to take off *now*! He had to be somewhere. He wasn't shy about letting us all know it! Even though he was several rows back, it sounded like he was right behind me.

I looked around and quietly observed what people were doing while this guy was having his fit. What I saw was interesting. There were a lot of older people sitting around me. A couple in one row read their books, another couple was talking and laughing with the couple seated in the row next to them, and another couple was reading the newspaper. Not one of them were fazed by Jim Bob's meltdown in row six. None seemed to be bothered, fazed, or even slightly distracted by all the commotion, or even by the delay. They appeared to be as happy and content as could be, just taking it all in stride.

After about an hour, we finally took off. The older couples were still happy, while Mr. Meltdown was still melting down. Even after we had arrived at our destination, and as we were getting off the plane, he continued making sure everyone knew exactly how unhappy he was. I guess he didn't realize we all were already very much aware of that fact.

I learned a lot on the tarmac that day. First of all, airplane coffee is really not good. Second, maintaining peace in any situation is totally up to us. If you think about it, the pilot couldn't change the situation. The guy and his loud complaints didn't change the circumstances. The only thing left to be altered was our attitudes. The older people were calm and refreshing. They were going to stay in a positive mindset and just enjoy the day, no matter what came their way. Jim Bob's frame of mind was annoying. He was bothered, angry, disrespectful, and downright agitated, and he wanted to make sure everyone else knew exactly how he felt about this situation. You know the old saying: misery loves company. Well, there you have it. Because he was perturbed, he made it his mission to try and surround himself with as much company as possible. The perturbed guy and the elderly couples sat on the same plane, but with very different attitudes.

The scripture says that God will give us power to keep ourselves calm in the days of adversity. (Psalm 94:13) Having a peaceful mindset is totally up to us. It's not about what's going on around us, it's all about what's going on *within* us. A mindset actually means that it is something that is "mine to set." The responsibility doesn't fall on other people, challenges, or obstacles. In the Bible, we're reminded to "Search for peace, and work to maintain it." (Psalm 34:14 NLT) Sometimes we may have to work hard to find peace, especially in the midst of chaos. And once we set our mind, we'll then have to make an effort to keep it set in a positive direction.

Practice and Promote Peace

You know when you don't have peace. It's painfully noticeable. You feel stressed, anxious, and unsure. In the same regard, a peaceful countenance is equally noticeable. Things happen around you, yet somehow, by the grace of God, you remain calm and sure because you have managed to set your mind. God's peace surpasses all understanding.

If you want peace to be the foundation of your life, then you'll have to learn how to master it. Along the way, you might have to make some adjustments. In my home, my state of mind sets the atmosphere. I have to have a peaceful mindset or things can go sideways in a hurry. The scripture says that a wise person builds their house, while the foolish tears theirs down by their own hands. (Proverbs 14:1) This verse is very powerful because it tells us that we have the power to erect or destroy. We have to make an effort to promote peace and continually work towards it.

If you've lost your peace because you're tired, then get some rest. If you're stressed and hungry, eat! If you're uptight because you and your spouse aren't spending enough time together, put the kids to bed early and have a date. (Remember, your kids are always watching, especially observing how spouses treat one another.)

Maybe, for you, peace comes from removing clutter. I get it. I'm one of those people who doesn't like clutter either because it tends to also clutter my mind—and then essentially my peace. Knowing this about myself, I try my best to regularly clear clutter. I do whatever it takes to keep things clean and picked up. Instead of complaining about it, I work towards what I know will bring me back to peace.

You may also have to protect your peace. If at all possible, opt out of conversations that aren't adding something good. If you can remove the negative, life instantly becomes more peaceful and ***better than ever***. Don't let others steal the peaceful environment that you've fought for. You don't have to participate in every argument. Choose peace. Don't allow others to pull you into their storm. Instead, see if you can pull them into your peace. Walk away from the drama.

Another alternative to allowing yourself to get all worked up over things is to consciously change your perspective. Maybe that delay in traffic means you were protected from an accident. Stay in peace and listen to the radio. Maybe waiting in that long line represents God opening the door for you to talk to someone. Stay in peace and keep your eyes open. Create a change in your way of thinking. If you can become positive, when all circumstances say you should be negative, you'll not only feel better, but you'll actually be ***better than ever***. You'll enjoy the day in a better way and, quite possibly, change other people's lives—just by being you! Master peace. And remember, if something costs your peace, then it's way too expensive.

YOUR PURSUIT

Concentrate on finding and holding on to peace to make your life better than ever. If a situation doesn't bring peace, exit it gracefully.

CHAPTER 26

Write Your Story

"My most important mission field is my family."

—JOHN OSTEEN

Oh, how I can remember waking up to the smell of coffee. Not just any coffee, but Daddy's coffee. I could smell that distinct, bold aroma the moment my sleepy eyes tried to open. As I ventured out of my room and headed towards the kitchen, I knew exactly what he would be doing. It was inevitable. Daddy would be sitting in his cozy chair in the den with a blanket, his Bible, and a freshly brewed cup of that wonderful-smelling, piping hot coffee. The scenario was a given in my house, as certain as the sun coming up every morning. If Daddy was home, this was his routine. He loved his coffee, his chair, and, oh yes, how he loved his Bible. This wasn't some religious ritual that he felt tied to every day. No. It was who he was. He would flip through that well-worn Bible of his like he was searching for a priceless treasure. He underlined the good parts, he quoted from it often, and, to the best of his ability, he lived its words daily.

Daddy loved people. And he sure loved God. He was the kind of man who never met a stranger. And as much as he loved the Lord, I also knew my dad loved us, his family, most. Did I mention I was his favorite? Haha. Although he's been in Heaven for quite some time now, the life lessons he taught me, and the rest of my family, were then, and remain, legacy lessons. These lessons shaped who I am now and who I will continue to become. They are the gifts that keep on giving (and the best thing my dad left to us all). For that I am grateful. His teachings and examples of how we are to be our best and strive to become ***better than ever*** every single day will always be with me. These lessons are the foundation on which I've grown. They inform and shape my actions and my reactions. I can think of no better way to pass on some of these lessons, other than to list a small fraction of them here:

- Never chase a boy. A boy should always chase you.
- Always cheer people on.
- Pay for somebody's meal at a restaurant.
- Admit your mistakes.
- Say you're sorry.
- Always give people the benefit of the doubt.
- Believe in someone else's dream.
- Whistle…it'll brighten your day.
- Always be willing to laugh at yourself.
- Sing…even if you can't carry a tune.
- Everybody deserves a chance.
- Everybody deserves love.
- Rules are never more important than relationships.
- Family is always first.
- Love your spouse.
- Don't be so heavenly-minded that you're no earthly good.
- Laugh, laugh, laugh!

- You're never too old to play.
- Say "ahhhhhh" when you drink your coffee…it just makes it taste better.
- Never give up on the prodigal…always believe the prodigal will come home.
- Fight for the underdog.
- Never forget where you came from.
- Invest in your kids.
- Make life count.
- Don't be ashamed of your imperfections.
- Follow your heart.
- Give people another chance…and another…and another.
- Always dress sharp.
- Walk with champions.
- You can never have too many shoes.
- Walk like you're ten feet tall.
- Love people, love people, love people.
- Be grateful.
- Stand up straight.
- Hold strong to what you believe.
- See the impossible.
- Lift the broken.
- Don't discount anyone because of their mistakes.
- Manage your money well.
- Invest in people.
- Live life.

- Say "I love you."
- Take time for people.
- Enjoy God's creation.
- Practice what you preach.
- Learn from your mistakes.
- Be happy.
- Pray like your life depends on it.
- Keep your priorities straight.
- Be on time...or better yet, a few minutes early.
- Keep it real.
- Be kind.
- Have fun.
- Take the high road.
- Keep your promises.

Even though my dad was a simple man, the impact he made was extraordinary. He didn't just preach what he believed, he lived it. He realized that kids were the bridge to the future, and he felt a great responsibility to pave the way for better days for each of us. He knew that it really didn't matter who someone thought you were, it only mattered that they remembered who you were.

Allow me to ask you this: What imprint will your life have made on others? We only get one shot at this thing called life. Let's make every single day count. Like it or not, your life will tell a story. Make sure it's a good one. I hope and pray you realize that how you live your life doesn't just affect you, but generations to come. Just think: you get to decide the memories and legacy you want to leave. Why not make them great ones? After all, inheritance is what you leave to someone, legacy is what you leave *inside* someone.

You're standing inside your legacy right now. You're the author of your story. Every day brings a fresh page. Now is the time to make your life ***better than ever***.

YOUR PURSUIT

Learn from the lessons taught by those you admire to evolve your life so that each day becomes *better than ever*.